MW00654782

THE URGING

OF CHRIST'S

LOVE

The Saints and The Social Teaching
of the Catholic Church

OMAR F. A. GUTIÉRREZ

Discerning Hearts
Omaha, Nebraska

Nihil Obstat
Rev. Matthew J. Gutowski, S.T.L.
Censor Deputatus

Imprimatur
+Archbishop George J. Lucas
Archbishop of Omaha
June 28, 2013

Discerning Hearts
Omaha, Nebraska
www.discerninghearts.com

© 2013 Omar F. A. Gutiérrez

ISBN 978-0988627024

ISBN 0988627027
All Rights Reserved

DEDICATION

To my wife Miriam, with whom I am blessed to
live the social teaching every day.

"This was the oath he swore
                 to our father Abraham:
to set us free from the hands of our enemies,
free to worship him without fear,
holy and righteous in his sight,
all the days of our life." Luke 1:73-75

CONTENTS

Acknowledgments   i

Forward   ii

Introduction   1

1 From Suffering to Sacrifice, St. Germaine Cousin   7

2 The Solitary Witness of Bl. Franz Jägerstätter   22

3 Liberation and St. Mary Magdalene   39

4 The Uncompromising St. Thomas More   58

5 The Selfless Heart of St. Jean Denaloue   79

6 Grace and Mercy, St. Maria Goretti   95

7 Sinner and Saint, St. Thomas Becket   109

8 Communion and St. Isidore of Seville   132

9 Salvation and Labor, St. Joseph the Workman   148

10 Running Like St. John   161

11 The Faith of Dorothy Day   174

End Notes   188

ACKNOWLEDGMENTS

I would like to acknowledge the patience and support of my family. I must especially thank Kris McGregor of Discerning Hearts. Kris has been a dear friend and a constant supporter. Without her, it can truly be said, this book would never have happened. I thank Deacon James Keating for his great generosity in writing a forward to this book. I am truly humbled by his kindness. I need to thank all the readers, and editors and commentators on the various drafts of this book: Rhonda Ortiz, Anna Dendinger and so many more. I must thank those prayer partners who helped to shepherd it along, especially those in the Pro Sanctity Movement. And I must thank my parents whose example provided me with so much of who and what I am. I cannot fail to thank the generosity of the Archdiocese of Omaha, and especially Archbishop George J. Lucas who has allowed me to work in the field of the social teaching of the Church.

I also need to thank the United States Conference of Catholic Bishops for the permission to reprint the portions of the Compendium of the Social Doctrine of the Catholic Church in the text below.

FORWARD

Here is the most unique book I have read in a long time. Through the lives of the saints we get a glimpse of what authentic spiritual integration is between holiness and doctrinal truth. Enfleshed in the saints, Omar Gutiérrez has discovered the true habitat for Catholic Social Teaching. The saints which are meditated upon in this work clearly show how being gifted with holiness has public consequences. Because one *is* holy one *is* just. Holiness is the love of God *received* and the love of God *given* as gift to the culture. Holiness does not create an isolated person statically gazing upon the Trinity in mystical paralysis. Holiness, instead, is a suffering of the Trinity's presence unto total, personal, moral and spiritual transformation. And because the transformation is so complete the saint *cannot help but give witness to the cause of his or her joy.*

This witness penetrates the secular arena. Holiness possesses social ramifications, and since it does, those who feel threatened by such holiness continually wish to dismiss lines as irrelevant to "modern" life. The holy one will not be dismissed, however. He or she will publically burn with love for God, embarrassing and challenging all those who simply want to enclose Christ in a church building for one hour on Sunday. Faith will not be limited to the socially and politically acceptable confines marked out by government, popular culture or the intellectual class. Religion is not private; it is as public as a man hanging upon a cross.

Within the pages of this book the reader will discover that it is love for God that ignites justice and all the virtues. Love for God is an endless fountain from which the saints stand and drink. As they drink of the Spirit their minds awaken to this truth: Man and God are not one. There is a barrier between man and God because of sin. Noting this reality the saint is urged on by the Spirit of Christ to enter a life of prophetic action. In other words God says to the saint, "Through my love and your suffering of my love unto the healing of your sins give witness to our relationship. Go to all those who still will not let Me reach them." Some saints take on the mission of Christ even at the cost of their own lives (martyrdom), but for all saints they take on His mission unto the death of their own egos.

In this way the saint is the only free man on the planet. He or she alone is bound so deeply to the mysteries of Christ they taste the freedom of no longer being torn by secular allegiances, tempted by idols, or tossed by the winds of cultural and political correctness. They embody the true man, men and women who have come to full stature, full maturity in Christ (Eph 4:13). It is the saint who is the only free person on the planet and therefore the only true adult. All the rest of us are still in high school wondering if the popular kids will ever notice us. Will I ever be "seen" by the powers of this passing world?

Meanwhile, the saints have quietly suffered a new identity, a second birth, a painful wrenching by the Spirit from all that undermines one's dignity and a joyful receiving of all that Divine consolation affords. In such a crucible it is ludicrous for the saint not to go public with his or her love; such endurance in the face of painful conversion was entered so that Christ could be *KNOWN by others*.

I am hoping that the many who read this book will begin to see what the Catholic Church has always taught: no one loves God or is loved by God as a private predilection. God's love is as public as a marriage and as demanding as the very truth of life's own meaning. The saints know this and live this because they fully know how superficial life is without God, while the life of publically witnessing to God's merciful love is compelling by its substantive beauty. The saints represented in this book see the beauty and publicly live in its truth. Let them guide you to live there as well through the inspiring message of this book.

Deacon James Keating, Ph.D.
Institute for Priestly Formation
Creighton University, Omaha. NE

INTRODUCTION

Anyone who takes the time to dive into the lives of the saints quickly realizes that sanctity never comes easily and that the ranks of saints include more than levitating mystics who seemingly have no connection with reality. Those who study the lives of the saints also realize that sanctity is never just a single moment at the end of a sharp sword. It is a slow process marked by years of habit and effort.

The lives of the saints are our lives. They lived the same things we do day in and day out. At times in circumstances not too much unlike ours. At other times in conditions much worse.

The saints are not human anomalies reckoned by the Almighty. They are us. The only difference is that they refused to settle with a half-hearted relationship with Jesus. They could not stand to love him by only feints and empty promises.

For this reason, the lives of the saints are often the best volumes of theological insight and practical know-how one could wish for. Studying them is beneficial for the Catholic who wishes to live as a Catholic. The saints are not just words on a page or intellectual inventions. They are real people with real stories who lived under real tribulations.

Their sufferings and moral quandaries are often familiar to us. They too had long conversations with themselves. They too argued about this or that path in life. They too spoke to spouses or friends about difficulties and pains. They too shared their greatest spiritual joys with the same.

Following their lives and examples can teach us everything we need to know about how to live out the faith in society. This is the central theme of this book: to look into the lives of the saints in order to help us understand how to live the social teaching of the Catholic Church.] In the process, I hope to show that what made the saints the saints and what makes them models of the social teaching of the Church is less about what they did and more about *why they did it*. You see, the social teaching is not just social welfare; it's an extension of a relationship.

Living the social teaching is a result of an encounter with Jesus Christ. It is this encounter with Jesus that is the root of a just life. Therefore, what we do is much more than mere social justice. Justice is the bare minimum after all. Christ's love for his people was not merely a matter of justice, as though we were owed his death on the cross. No, the encounter with Christ provides a model of mercy and love that meets the requirements of justice but ultimately transcends them to reveal the power of a loving God who "lifts up the lowly and fills the hungry with good things."

This encounter with Jesus creates an urging, a drive, an impetus in the Christian (2 Cor. 5:14). Born of Christ's love, this urging is what differentiates the work of the saint from the work of the social worker, and so is the difference between the social teaching and secular humanism. The urging of Christ's love compels the Christian to share that love with others, to serve the poor because Christ loves the poor so much. And it is this urging that gives the saint the power to do the radically good thing when the wisdom of the world calls it folly.

Through the urging of Christ's love, we are dead to our own selfishness and fear and anxiety and are rather drawn to bless our neighbor by loving them as Jesus did. This is well more than social justice. This is more than building a just society. This is a matter of becoming agents of God to bring about a civilization of love.

The lives of the saints included in these pages are stories of human persons who, as you will see, struggle with many if not all of the same things we confront today. Human nature is human nature is human nature. Readers will hopefully see themselves in several of the saints included in this book and be encouraged to pursue sanctity themselves.

Of course, one of the great difficulties of today is not so much that Catholics do not believe they are called to holiness but that they believe they are already holy. Sanctity has, it seems, been dumbed down to be synonymous with being socially conscious, civil to our acquaintances and having avoided killing anyone. It is a low standard, the low road to heaven.

The truth is, though, that we are not called to be any less holy than the saints. Sanctity is sanctity is sanctity. Readers will hopefully be inspired to raise the bar on their own definitions of holiness as they read about these good and holy people in this book.

The saints included in the following are certainly not exhaustive of those that have something to show us about the social teaching. They were chosen without any other forethought than that some of them are my favorite, some of them are unknown – and so tantalizing in their newness – and some of them provide me with the opportunity to write about a certain aspect of the social teaching.

My sincere hope is that if you have not met one or two of them, you might find a new friend in heaven to whom to pray. I hope too that the reader can learn how to apply the lessons of the saint's life to his or her own. The goal is to learn from the saint about living the social teaching every day. In that way, we might draw closer to Jesus, and by drawing closer to him, we might become holier ourselves.

At the heart of the social teaching of the Catholic Church, and the way that the average Catholic begins to live it out in the real world, is this urging that comes from a deeply personal relationship with the God who is love. Paying attention to how we foster that relationship is the work of every Christian. Responding to the constant invitations that flow from that relationship is to live the social teaching.

At the end of every chapter, I invoke the saint's name and Christ the King. Pope Pius XI, who gave us the second great social encyclical and is, with Pope Leo XIII, the parent of many of the principles of the social teaching, also gave us the Feast of Christ the King.

I include a praise of Christ the King because as Catholics we transcend political partisanship and party loyalty. Or at least we ought to. We have our one true sovereign already. Invoking him is a reminder to all of us that conservative, liberal, libertarian, or progressive, social democrat, green, originalist, or independent do not enter into these discussions about the social teaching. We are simply Catholic, and we have one loyalty, and that is to Christ Jesus. So long live Christ the King!

I have also included a prayer which the reader can use to draw themselves into a relationship with that saint. And I have included a quote from the *Compendium of the Social Doctrine of the Catholic*

Church. The *Compendium* was promulgated in 2005 by the Pontifical Council for Justice and Peace at the Vatican. It is a great resource for those who want to learn more about the social teaching. I encourage everyone to purchase a copy for their home as a reference work or to access it online at the Vatican website.

One final note on the last chapter on Dorothy Day. Ms. Day is not a saint but she has been proclaimed a Servant of God by the Church. I have included her, however, just as I included Blessed Franz, because she has a lot to teach us. I have placed her last in the book because through her I think I can better comment on those who teach/preach social justice today. I suspect that she would not be pleased by all that is done in the name of the Church's social teaching. I suspect she would call for more formation for those who want to work for the poor. I'm also sure she would love all those who sincerely work for the "littlest of these".

Omar F. A. Gutiérrez

I

FROM SUFFERING TO SACRIFICE, ST. GERMAINE COUSIN

Every June 15th the Church remembers a saint who, though little known, ought to become a personal favorite. It is not because she is a wonderful mystic, though no doubt on some level she was. And it is not because she expressed herself in such eloquent language. She never wrote a word. St. Germaine Cousin is remarkable because, when we think about her story, one wants to weep, much like we imagine St. Peter did when he realized that he had betrayed Christ's love.

St. Germaine does with blinding perfection what a saint is supposed to do: to reflect Jesus into the world and to us, so that we can come to know what living as a Christian really means.

A Daughter of Suffering

St. Germaine was born in 1579 to a peasant family in Pibrac in south-western France just a few miles West of Toulouse. This is an interesting part of the world, smack dab in the middle of the neck that connects Spanish Iberia to France and the European continent.

Toulouse, by the way, is where in 721 AD one-hundred thousand Muslims attempted to establish their foothold in Europe but were beaten back by Frankish armies. Toulouse is where the Moorish invasion was stopped for a time, allowing Charles Martel to save Europe from Islamic conquest eleven years later at Tours. Perhaps because many forget their history, many forget that the Francs were some of the toughest people on the face of the planet, tough and brutal. Poor little Germaine knew very well about that brutality.

She was the daughter of Laurent Cousin and of Marie Laroche. Her mother died when Germaine was still just a baby. She was born with a deformed and weak right hand and developed lymphadenitis, which causes large but benign masses to form at the neck. These tumors could grow quite large and turn blue and purple. "Unsightly" is too mild a word for the condition.

Germaine's father and her new stepmother viewed these infirmities as excuses to treat their daughter as less than human. She was forced to sleep in the barn or under the stairs without a proper bed, having only straw. She was fed after the family meal with the scraps left over. She was subject to beatings and scalding with boiling water if she made a mistake, real or imagined.

Her parents feared that her disease was contagious, so she was not allowed to interact with the other, "healthy" children. They insisted that she spend her days tending the sheep off in the fields. Though we often have a romanticized notion of shepherds, it was low-skilled labor and was situated away from town. It was a task suitable for children or social outcasts. Germaine was both. It is hard to imagine from these early details that she ever heard a kind word from her family.

So far, we see in Germaine the suffering heart of a child. In our own world there are many who suffer as badly, whose pains include terribly cruel and violent rejections. We even see unintended rejections which are no less painful in young hearts that grow weary with the hidden ache. Worse, there are many whose lives are snuffed out before they are even allowed what Germaine was allowed. Many parents kill their children in the womb when they find out that the child is "deformed."

It is said that some 90% of pregnancies end in abortion when Down Syndrome is diagnosed in the unborn child. The brutality of Germaine's parents is horrid, but perhaps we are no less brutal than those Francs after all? Whatever the case, this is a particularly difficult beginning for the life of a saint.

We would not be surprised if the little French girl would grow bitter against her parents, against the world and – for good measure – against God for putting her in the state that she was in: deformed, ill, abused, poor, lonely, forgotten.

Today's atheists would certainly mock the self-deluded little Germaine for being so stupid as to believe in a God that allows her to suffer. And if ever there were an argument for the atheist, Germaine's life is it. Like Dostoevsky's character Ivan Karamazov, the brother who rejected God because of the suffering of children, the modern atheist could certainly use Germaine's story as evidence that God is irrelevant. He is pointless if such a girl can be allowed to suffer so much. Yet this French lass loved God and did so in a manner that puts us to shame.

Alternatively, if her story were told today by Hollywood, there is very little doubt that eventually Germaine would be portrayed as a fiery avenger. With spectacular gymnastics and while wielding spinning swords and daggers, she would certainly murder her parents and their accomplices. She would be remembered by some catch phrase that proves her toughness. Her vigilante justice and her rejection of society and its backward morality would make her adored by the masses. That is the way Hollywood would present her story. But this is not Germaine's story. The lives of the saints are about reality, not Hollywood.

The reality was that in the midst of her

suffering, Germaine found a great comfort in the natural world that surrounded her. There she found the quiet and still voice of the Almighty. She found reality and God in the fields in which she watched the sheep. Her time there provided the opportunity to commune with the Creator, and she rested in this relationship with him. She prayed the rosary constantly, and, by meditating on their lives, grew ever closer to Mary and to Jesus.

Instead of bitterness at her condition in life, she found herself overjoyed at being alive in Christ. Instead of casting curses to the heavens, she gazed up at them and was reminded by the twinkling stars of the love that God had for her and just for her. Who are we, then, who curse the Lord for far lesser problems? Despite all her suffering, she could still praise the gentle love of God, the Creator of the universe.

Now none of this is to suggest that abuse is okay or to be ignored in order to achieve holiness. Nothing could be further from the truth. A righteous anger would be normal. But this is precisely why the grace we find in St. Germaine ought to be so arresting to our consciences. The saints are supposed to inspire us beyond the merely normal. In the way Germaine deals with her suffering, she proves the power of grace and the power of God's love, inspiring us to strive for an ever greater love.

The Pious Girl

Germaine never missed an opportunity to go to Mass. When she would hear the bells for Mass ring, she would plant her shepherd's staff in the ground, tell her guardian angel to watch over the sheep and would run to Mass. She never lost a single sheep, though that part of the world is known for its wolves.

On one occasion, according to the reports of the people of the town, there was a great rain storm that swelled the stream separating her fields from the church. This did not stop Germaine. God parted the waters of the stream so that his little girl could come visit him.

This brings up another interesting aspect of her life. Neighbors are fickle creatures. On one hand they are apt to treat people in the same manner as the family treats them. The people of Pibrac usually treated Germaine as her parents did. They ridiculed her, ignored her, berated her. Interestingly, even as they saw her in constant prayer or running to Mass, they made fun of her piety. Though they were Catholics themselves, they found her devotion just a bit much.

We have probably seen something similar today. We need no imagination for what it looks like when society, or even a fellow Catholic, pokes fun at our piety. An ever-so-slight shake of the head, an almost inaudible tisk-tisk or the snide comment uttered under one's breath can betray someone else's disapproval of our devotion. Zeal for the Catholic faith, for the whole and entire Catholic faith, is definitely not in style in America. Unabashedly living with authenticity is not welcome in our society. So it was in Pibrac, in a way and at least for a time, that Germaine's piety was seen as another sign of her "problem."

It is good for us to think about this, however. Do we allow ourselves to be cowed by those who think us too pious? Do we avoid the comment that reveals our faith to the fellow at work or to the comrade waiting in the doctor's office? Do we shudder at the thought of actually praying in public, saying grace in a restaurant, offering a prayer to a suffering colleague? If we do, we ought to remember poor little Germaine.

Still, and this is the rest of the story, despite their initial ridicule of the girl, Germaine's neighbors found it harder and harder to ignore her constancy. She *never* missed Mass. She *never* retaliated against those who abused her, though she had opportunity. She *never* spoke ill of her parents who, they all knew, were a bit too harsh with the girl. "Why should they treat her thus?" they began to think, "She's just a cripple after all." Eventually, even the hardened heart can be touched by piety lived with loving abandon.

The town's folk also noted that, while she did not have friends amongst the girls her own age, Germaine did have the habit when she was older of gathering the children of the town around her to teach them basics of the faith, even though she couldn't read. When one spends all day and night meditating on the lives of the Blessed Virgin and Our Lord, one can imagine remarkable settings for the stories of their lives and foster great intimacy with the two of them. It was the insight from this constant meditation that she used with the children. She would tell them the stories of Jesus and of Our Lady, helping the children encounter the Holy Family personally.

So it was that this sickly, handicapped, ostracized girl of rural France could teach children their faith without books or curricula or videos. She did it without certifications, felt banners, flash cards, pageants or PhD's. Certainly the children of today are different from the children of 16th century France, but they are the same in that children respond to passion. Children respond to those who love, to those who know Jesus as a friend, to those who share conversations with him every day. Germaine has much to suggest to our contemporary catechists.

Miracle

One day in the deepest part of winter, which can be quite harsh in France, Germaine's stepmother chased her out of the house with a stick, threatening to beat her. She was accused of stealing some scraps of bread hidden in her apron. Of course, she had never stolen a thing in her life, but that is beside the fact. She is accused of stealing bread from her own father's table. We should recall here the line from Sacred Scripture, "Which of you, if your child asks for bread, will give him a stone?" (Mt 7:9) The violence here is physical and psychological and spiritual. Germaine was older now, in her twenties, but she was still her father's child. It is difficult to imagine the kind of pain she must have felt at being denied food and then being accused falsely.

The neighbors witnessed this scene. They had begun to think of Germaine as a holy child of God. Unable to write her off as a kook anymore, some almost stepped in. But they stopped themselves because of what they saw.

When, with the force of one caught up in unthinking anger, the stepmother tugged violently at the apron around Germaine's waste, it opened wide. Instead of bread falling out to accuse this child against her parents, out fell a stream of *summer* flowers. One ought to imagine the scene: yellow day lilies and the purple phlox and the crimson poppies falling and alighting on the snowy ground. It was this miracle that finally broke the icy coldness of the parents' hearts, much the same way that Juanito's roses, given to him by the lovely Lady of Guadalupe, broke the power of Aztec terror on the other side of the world just a few decades before.

Germaine's parents, now aware of their terrible behavior, invited their daughter to come to sleep in a proper bedroom within the home, not under the stairs on straw. St. Germaine declined. She was happy with the simple life she had lived, though it would not last much longer.

Shortly after this moment with the flowers, at the age of only twenty-two, Germaine died sleeping on the straw underneath the stairs in the Cousin house. The year was 1601. She was buried in the local Church and, when during a renovation in 1644 her body was accidentally exhumed, she was discovered to be perfectly preserved. She was moved to a leaden coffin and placed in the sacristy of the Church. Sixteen years later, she was seen again and was again found to be incorrupt.

During the anti-Catholic persecutions of the French Revolution, her body was stolen by a man named Toulza, who threw quick-lime and water on the body in order to destroy it. That seems almost too fitting. The atheist can only respond to such a beautiful soul with that kind of demonic hatred. I suppose Germaine would have us pray for his soul. Happily, most of the body was later discovered to be intact, damaged but intact. Because of the Revolution, there was a delay in her cause, but she was ultimately canonized by Pope Pius IX in 1867.

From Suffering to Sacrifice

Now, as if all of this were not enough, there is still more to St. Germaine's life to which we should pay attention. Despite the very little food she was given by her family, the food she was accused of "stealing" that winter's day, Germaine always did her best to share what she had with those in need. This young, French girl whom our own society would say was cursed with disease and deformity, this girl found the goods of this earth not important at all. Instead of seeking a much-deserved comfort, she wished to spend her time in service of the King of Glory. So she gave her bread to the poor who had nothing, just as her Lord had asked. What little she did receive she gave away in acts of love. This is crucially important.

Through those moments of self-gift, Germaine transformed the unjust suffering that turns our stomachs into acts of sacrifice that liberate and inspire us. She turned the tables on the devil and all that is evil. She exemplifies the great glory of the Christian life that gives meaning to human suffering. Like Jesus, who was likewise unjustly treated, Germaine transformed the ugliness of man's hate for other men into an opportunity to glorify the Father.

Thus, despite her own predicament, in giving to the poor and ministering to those who struggle to survive, Germaine ceases to be the victim of her parents' and society's brutality. She becomes the powerful *belle femme* who stands athwart history and human hatred saying, "Christ has freed me to love, and love conquers all things." Through her movement from suffering to sacrifice, she is transformed before our very eyes from victim to heroine.

Hers is not the Hollywood version with flashy hair styles and physical derring-do. In a kind of stupefying paradox of Christian witness, she reveals that she is truly free who can freely give. Complete freedom is the ability to deny self for the sake of the other, to give oneself as gift. This girl had the quiet strength that proves it. She did this through acts of charity, and charity in truth is what makes us whole and healthy. In her selfless gifts to the poor, she revealed herself to be, despite her outward appearance, the healthiest person in Pibrac. It is precisely in her brokenness that the truth is finally revealed.

No doubt there are single mothers where you are. There are heads of families who have to choose between fuel for getting to work or for electricity to keep the little food they have. There are families whose parents have lost both their jobs and who are struggling to discover what to do.

While some of us consider whether or not to vacation here or there, some, despite their best efforts, are trying to figure out how to get to an interview so that they can work. While feelings of frustration well up in our breast over not being able to purchase this or that seemingly important thing, there are some who have been abandoned by their spouses in the name of the contemporary freedoms. Wounded lovers and children litter the horizon. They are so common we might not even notice them anymore. But St. Germaine Cousin, the little girl from France, notices them. She gave to the poor not out of material wealth but out of the riches of love she had for Christ the King. Could we do the same? Can we give out of love?

Remember too that St. Germaine does not stand before us to scold. She wants to gather us around her, as she did with the little children, and tell us about Jesus and Mary. Her injured body aches to tell us how much Our Lord and his Mother love us and want to help us love others.

St. Germaine does not stand before us to judge but to invite us into the relationship she enjoyed with Christ. From that place, then, we can better discern how best to use our wealth for the greatest good. We remember, in the meantime, that St. Germaine gave from her want and found strength in her giving. She yearns to let us know that, as we discern how to budget our charitable work and donations, Christ is there to guide and call us to more, even to sacrifice.

St. Germaine Cousin of Pibrac pray for us. And may Jesus and Mary, our King and Queen, live and rule in our hearts forever.

Prayer

St. Germaine, though rejected by the world, you still found the strength to love without boundary, to give without being mindful of your own needs, to trust in a good God who loves us all so deeply. In the midst of our struggles with our own wounds of rejection, wounds that can consume us, help us to trust as you did.

Pray to the Father that we may learn what it is to know the unconditional love which he offers us and to learn gratitude for all the gifts we have been given. Help us to overcome our feelings of rejection by trusting in his love.

We ask also, dear Germaine, that you teach us the ways of Jesus and Mary as you did the little children who came to you. We so long to know them as you do. Pray for us dear Germaine that we might begin to have your same simplicity of heart. Pray that we can forgive as you did. Pray that when we feel rejected we can always turn to the Father and enjoy his everlasting embrace. Amen.

The Compendium

148. *Persons with disabilities are fully human subjects, with rights and duties*: ...

The rights of persons with disabilities need to be promoted with effective and appropriate measures: "It would be radically unworthy of man, and a denial of our common humanity, to admit to the life of the community, and thus admit to work, only those who are fully functional. To do so would be to practice a serious form of discrimination, that of the strong and healthy against the weak and sick."[1]

359. …One must never forget "the duty of charity …, that is, the duty to give from one's 'abundance', and sometimes even out of one's needs, in order to provide what is essential for the life of a poor person."[2]

II

THE SOLITARY WITNESS OF
BLESSED FRANZ JÄGERSTÄTTER

Linz is in upper Austria, and in the soil and water of Linz and its surrounding villages and towns, amidst the rolling hills that ease up and down along the Salzach and Inn rivers, there is something that seems to make men zealous, willful and energetic. At times this has been a bad thing for the world. Adolph Eichmann, one of the architects of the Holocaust, was brought up in Linz. Adolph Hitler was born in Braunau am Inn, along the Inn River which flows into the Salzach. But in the case of one man remembered by the Church every August 9th, this peculiar Austrian zeal exemplifies for us the social teaching of the Church in stunningly stark form.

The Wild One

Born in the village of St. Radegund just 21 miles from Brauanau am Inn, Franz Jägerstätter was the illegitimate child of Franz Bachmeier and Elisabeth Huber. The father was killed during the First World War, the war to end all wars, and in 1917 Elisabeth married Heinrich Jägerstätter who quickly adopted the young lad.

Franz was a good school boy by all accounts, scoring well in math and history and very well in writing and religion. As a young man, however, he was a bit of a wild one. In fact "The Wild One," the 1953 film starring Marlon Brando, is exactly appropriate, since it was Franz who first introduced his small village to the motorcycle.

Franz was in the habit of drinking too much at the pub. He gambled quite a bit. He was a hard worker, but he played hard too. He was prone to getting into fights with the young men in neighboring villages, and he did enjoy pursuits of the fairer sex.

In his biography of Franz Jägerstätter, *In Solitary Witness*, Gordon C. Zahn notes how the villagers remembered their late Radegundian. Jägerstätter's wild youth was recalled with fondness, as one of the better aspects of the man. He was extolled for his spirited fun-making. He was considered a "great guy," easy to be around, outgoing and the life of parties. He was a leader amongst his group of friends and was well liked for his joviality.

In 1933, Franz fathered a child, a girl who would grow up to be Hildegard Auer. This was not the rarest of things in St. Radegund. Zahn relates that families in this part of the world, and in that era, would sometimes encourage daughters to secure a good marriage by allowing such a thing to happen. At other times, youth would deliberately get pregnant in order to force a family to recognize a relationship and hand over the family holdings. Marriage was not always required, but certainly a young man couldn't just leave the girl alone to raise the child by herself. This is, sadly, precisely what Franz did when he left town.

Was he trying to escape responsibility? Was he driven out by the other young men of the town for this indiscretion? Or was it some other problem or feud that sent him packing? It is not clear what the motivation was, and there is some question as to whether or not he was even the father. What is known is that he left, worked in the mines, made some money and that when he returned he was a different man.[3]

By 1935 he was more diligent about prayer. He educated himself about the faith by reading Scripture and borrowing books from the parish. He faithfully attended the adult education class offered by the pastor. In 1936 he decided to adopt a full and complete devotion to his faith, one that meant that he would be Catholic in everything that he said and did. He would allow his faith to permeate every aspect of his life. In this way, he demonstrates the meaning of Catholic social teaching.

Like any doctrine from Mother Church, the social teaching aims to show us the path to heaven. That path involves living our faith in every aspect and activity and not just on Sundays or in those moments which please us. Catholic social teaching is about thoroughly living an authentic Christian life. Franz pursued this life passionately. He would no longer be a "half-way" Christian who feigns at devotion and does not allow the waters of faith to feed his interior desert. Christ would, he hoped, embrace him in the end and not spit him out for being lukewarm.

The Fanatic

In that same year of 1936, Franz married Franziska Schwanginger, a devout Catholic woman. After the wedding, the two traveled to Rome for their honeymoon, a rare adventure for humble peasant farmers from Upper Austria. They arrived in Rome and received a papal blessing for their marriage. These events solidified the zealous love for the faith that Franz had been cultivating.

It is at this point that the villagers, in their re-telling of Franz's life, begin to grumble a bit at the religious "fanaticism" of their neighbor. He would sing hymns while gathering hay. He would take breaks during the day to say a prayer or two, or perhaps to read a holy text. He would fast in the mornings until he could receive Holy Communion at the noon Mass – a significant feat considering how early farmers get up and how hard they work in the morning.

He stopped gambling and would not play at cards unless it was agreed that no money would be exchanged. He stopped frequenting the pubs. This was not because he believed alcohol immoral, but because he wished to avoid the inevitable arguments over politics. The National Socialists were all the rage in Germany, and talk of the Nazi party was creeping over into Austria.

To the villagers, Franz's new piety was all madness. Indeed, some of them claimed that he was mentally deranged, which is an interesting point to ponder. It was the personal and open devotion of this simple man that was called madness by the town-folk. While the winds of war were beginning to blow hard and hot over the Austrian landscape, piety was madness. While Hitler and Mussolini signed a compact, while the German Führer planned to annex Austria, Franz's singing to the Blessed Virgin while forking hay was considered lunacy.

Is it not the case that the piety of others may make their neighbors uncomfortable? Are we often afraid of praying in public? What do people think of us who live our faith so openly?

Franz's "lunacy" would begin to affect his life most acutely when, in 1938, Germany announced the *Anschluss*, or the "link-up," between Germany and Austria. The move by Hitler to annex Austria was opposed by Chancellor Kurt Schuschnigg, who tried to rally the people of Austria towards a referendum against unification. However, Hitler would have none of it. He effectively invaded Austria in March. A referendum among the Austrian population, held in April of that year, gave nearly 100% support to the German take-over. One of the few who voted against it was Franz Jägerstätter.

In fact, Franz was the only man in his town to vote against the *Anschluss*. He believed the Nazi party to be a great evil and a harm against the Church. In perhaps one of the saddest moments for the Catholic Church during the real madness of the Second World War, Cardinal Innitzer of Vienna supported the unification and encouraged Catholics to vote for it. The Cardinal believed that Germany would respect the Catholic Church, which had far more influence in Austria than she did in Germany, and that anything was better than the Communist influences from the East.

But the peasant farmer from St. Radegund knew better. He knew that Hitler was no friend of the Church and that he would destroy all that he touched. Jägerstätter compared the actions of the Austrian Church to that of the Jews who chose Barabbas over our own dear Lord. Innitzer would of course learn to regret his decision.[4]

In the years following these events, Franz Jägerstätter would shout in a solitary voice against the Nazi regime every chance he got, even refusing their money. One of the fascinating aspects of Jägerstätter's life, and one that ought to give us great pause as we consider public policy, is his rejection of State welfare.

Franz argued that this new State authority did not have the right to try to feed the poor or care for the widows in St. Radegund. This was the responsibility, so he argued, of the people and not the State. Though his own family did not live well, Franz would gather food stuffs and personally deliver them to the poor so that they would not have to take the tainted "charity" of the Nazi government.

He wrote once, "Anyone who wishes to practice Christian charity in his deeds can manage to provide the poor with something for their sustenance without" such State intervention.[5]

Franz Jägerstätter would also refuse emergency farm grants after a hailstorm. He rejected the advance of the Nazi Folk Community, the Winter Relief Collection and the People's Welfare Fund. He could be called the Apostle of Subsidiarity in that he resisted the imposition of the State, the national socialist state, on the lives of Christians whose responsibility it was to care for the poor and widowed. Under the Nazi regime, however, the Church could have no role. The socialist State required control of all benefices and so required that the Church stay out of it.

The Man of Conscience

In 1940 Franz became a third order Franciscan and the sacristan for his parish. Amusingly, he would close the church doors as soon as Mass started in order to force those who showed up late to go through the embarrassing task of having to knock and be let in. Also, sick of the gossip that would take place before and after Mass, Franz barred everyone from the sacristy who did not need to be there. In the boldness of his nature, he would also advise his pastor about what to say in the homilies. He encouraged the priest to talk more about the dangers of hell in order to motivate the people into a deeper devotion for the Lord. His pastor often took the advice.

It was also in 1940 that Franz was called up to serve in the Nazi army. At first he did respond to the call. He went through basic training but was given a waiver to return to St. Radegund. This may have been because of his age, the fact that he now had three daughters or that he was a farmer. Whatever the reason, when he returned after the short military training, he began to seek the advice of priests and his bishop about whether it was moral for him to fight for this unjust regime and in their unjust war.

They all, to a man, would say later that Franz's arguments were clear and logical. He would lay out the moral reasoning with precision and passion. He ought not and could not fight for the

German side. This was a man in complete control of his faculties. Yet each of them would say to Franz that he had to consider the needs of his family, his wife and three daughters. Each of them would tell him that he had duties to the State and that he could join the German effort through other means, but Franz was never convinced.

On February 22nd, 1943 Franz Jägerstätter was called up for military service by the German high command. He traveled to Enns to report for duty, all the way weighing in his mind and heart what he was to do. How could he leave his family behind? Would there be retribution against them? How could he turn his back on Christ? Ought not perfection be the goal of the spiritual life?

On March 1st, after consulting a young priest who did not impress him, Franz told the military attaché that he would not fight. He was arrested immediately and taken to Linz. He wrote many letters to his wife in the attempt to console her and to give the family advice about farming the land. He was greatly pained for his family. Still, he was sure his decision was the right one. He notes in a statement to the prison chaplain:

> "Again and again people stress the obligations of conscience as they concern my wife and children. Yet I cannot believe that, just because one has a wife and children, he is free to offend God by lying. Did not Christ Himself say, 'He who loves father, mother, or children

more than me is not deserving of My love'? Or, 'Fear not those who can kill the body but not the soul; rather fear much more those who seek to destroy body and soul in hell.'"[6]

This is quite the testimony for us today. Franz challenges our regular habit of rationalizing every sin. Are we Christians or are we not? Certainly family is important, but should family get in the way of the pursuit of sanctity? Is this not what Jesus warned against?

It is important to note that one does not read in Franz's letters much vitriol. There is no visceral call for political overthrow or bloody revolution. Jägerstätter believed he was simply responding to Christ's call to be holy, to be virtuous, to live the Gospel in full.

In a letter to his godson he wrote, "I can say from my own experience how painful life often is when one lives as a half-way Christian; it is more like vegetating than living."[7] This line gives us a sense of the zeal found in Franz, the passion that made up his character. He was a man in full control of his life and was directing that life towards Christ. To live by this creed meant living it completely. So perhaps we must ask a more fundamental question: is it zeal to live consistently and with integrity? Is one a zealot merely because one desires to live their life as they say they believe?

It is also important to emphasize that Franz Jägerstätter is not the example of a political dissident who deliberately gets arrested to prove a point. He did not seek to be arrested. He only submitted himself to arrest after being confronted by the choice. Franz was not a radical idealist "sticking it to the man." He was a man in love with Christ Jesus, who only wanted to authentically live the Christian life. In his case, he found that in Nazi Austria this could not be done.

Despite all that afflicted him, Franz still sought holiness in prison. For example, in a letter to his wife, he asks her to send him some edelweiss, the national flower of Austria. It seemed a fellow inmate from France wanted to send some of this lovely white flower to his girlfriend back home.[8] This little act of kindness to another inmate demonstrates the humanity of Franz almost better than anything else. In the midst of his trial he thinks of others and encourages his family to do so as well.

In July he was moved to Berlin, stood trial and was quickly convicted. On August 9th, 1943 he was beheaded by guillotine. He was only 36 years old.

His family survived the war, though they suffered much. The villagers looked after them to a degree. They chalked up Franz's fate to the consequences of lunacy and religious dogmatism. He was not considered a hero by the people of St. Radegund but rather as an irresponsible man who failed to take proper care of his family. A father's role, they argued, is to support his wife and children. Is not that a pro-life position, too?

There is surely some part of us that would agree with this assessment. Did not his children have a right to a life with their father? Did not his wife have the right to the aid of her husband in raising three children and providing for them? These are reasonable arguments, but Franz Jägerstätter saw it differently. He believed he was winning for his family a far greater wealth, providing his children with a far finer figure than any old father. He was gifting them with the image of what a Christian father looks like. For this reason, if not for many others, the life of Blessed Franz Jägerstätter is sobering.

He wrote once:

"Therefore we must do everything in our power to strive toward the Eternal Homeland and to preserve a good conscience. Then, even if our enemies attack us and even if they are armed, they will not be able to tear us away from this Homeland. Though we must bear our daily sorrows and reap little reward in this world for doing so, we can still become richer than millionaires – for those who need not fear death are the richest and happiest of all. And these riches are there for the asking."[9]

Thus, in the midst of the Nazi love for the German homeland, the land of the racially pure people, Franz Jägerstätter kept his eyes on the eternal homeland of heaven where all are invited and all are beautiful and all are loved. He understood the true wealth of the Kingdom of God, where Christ is King and the evil of the Nazi power is but a nuisance. He exemplifies what can happen to the authentic Christian in the community of the world, the world that rejects the Holy Spirit because it cannot see the Holy Spirit. Here is what he wrote about Christian persecution:

"Since the death of Christ, almost every century has seen the persecution of Christians; there have always been heroes and martyrs who gave their lives – often in horrible ways – for Christ and their faith. If we hope to reach our goal someday, *then we too must become heroes of the faith*. For as long as we fear men more than God, we will never make the grade. O this cowardly fear of men! Because of a few jeering words spoken by our neighbor, all our good intentions are thrown overboard. Of course even the most courageous and best Christians can and will fall, but they will not lie for long in the filth of sin. Instead they will pull themselves together and draw new strength from the sacraments of Penance and Holy Communion and strive on to their goal. And should anxious days come upon us when we feel we are being crushed under the weight of our troubles, let us remember that God burdens none of us with a heavier cross than he can bear."[10]

Let us remember that each of us is called to be a hero for the faith. Let us beware the inaction in our lives because of a "few jeering words spoken by our neighbor." Let us be willing to speak out against the evils of our time regardless of how intolerant or crazy we might seem to our neighbor. Twisted logics that justify voting for a man who defends infanticide or unjust war must not enter our minds. Let us all be willing to refuse cooperation with the evil of any political party or ideology so that we can rather be better subjects of Christ our King. Thanks be to him for giving us Blessed Franz Jägerstätter, whom we ask to pray for us.

Prayer

Dear Franz, though we do not face the choices you faced in your time, let us remember you when we fear pain or embarrassment. When we turn from the difficult call of the Christian life and choose rather the promises of the world, remind us of your witness. Guard us from a failure of prudence. Intercede for us if we become judgmental of others. Teach us to be a witness, even a solitary witness, and to do so with kindness and not anger, patience and not presumption, a joyful heart and not a cynical spirit.

Most of all dear Franz, help us to love our Lord as you did. We desire to be close to him and to live as citizens of his kingdom. Help us to be citizens of the Kingdom of God before we are members of any other party, group or nation. Pray for us, Franz, that we might be wholly and uncompromisingly Catholic. Amen.

The Compendium

187. *"The principle of subsidiarity protects people from abuses by higher-level social authority and calls on these same authorities to help individuals and intermediate groups to fulfill their duties. ... "*

The principle of subsidiarity is opposed to certain forms of centralization, bureaucratization, and welfare assistance and to the unjustified and excessive presence of the State in public mechanisms. "By intervening directly and depriving society of its responsibility, the Social Assistance State leads to a loss of human energies and an inordinate increase of public agencies, which are dominated more by bureaucratic ways of thinking than by concern for serving their clients, and which are accompanied by an enormous increase in spending".[11]....

In order for the principle of subsidiarity to be put into practice there is a *corresponding need* for: respect and effective promotion of the human person and the family; ever greater appreciation of associations and intermediate organizations in their fundamental choices and in those that cannot be delegated to or exercised by others; the encouragement of private initiative so that every social entity remains at the service of the common good, each with its own distinctive characteristics; the presence of pluralism in society and due representation of its vital components; safeguarding human rights and the rights of minorities; bringing about bureaucratic and administrative decentralization; striking a balance between the public and private spheres, with the resulting recognition of the *social* function of the private sphere; appropriate methods for making citizens more responsible in actively "being a part" of the political and social reality of their country.

500. *"A war of aggression is intrinsically immoral. ..."*

It is important to remember that "it is one thing to wage a war of self-defense; it is quite another to seek to impose domination on another nation. The possession of war potential does not justify the use of force for political or military objectives. Nor does the mere fact that war has unfortunately broken out mean that all is fair between the warring parties".[12]

III

LIBERATION AND
ST. MARY MAGDALENE

St. Mary Magdalene is the patroness of contemplatives, converts, penitent sinners and evangelists.
Her feast day is July 22nd, and it is the same day as
my father's passing. There is a kind of bittersweet
comfort in knowing that he died on this day, as my
father was for the majority of his life a decided
atheist.

As a young man, he was caught up in the
revolutionary spirit of Latin America, the Castro
revolution and the infatuations with socialism. Like
some proponents of a kind of liberation theology,
my father considered Karl Marx a great thinker.
The struggle of life was a struggle of classes.
Everything boiled down to that. Marxism sees at
the heart of the human experience the dissonance
caused by the gap between the haves and the have-
nots.

Liberation, then, is freedom from socio-economic difference and thus oppression. It is only possible through the acquisition of power. Freedom is self-determination. History is the result of man's will. Salvation is earthly peace. Justice is an end to the system. This is Marxism. It is not, however, the teaching of the Church or the lesson about liberation which we learn from St. Mary Magdalene.

Before we get too far into Mary's life, some distinctions need to be made about who this woman was. There is the story in Sacred Scripture of the woman who, Pharisees watching on, bathed the feet of Christ with her tears before she covered them in expensive ointment (Luke 7:37-50). She is not named but only referred to as "a sinful woman in the city." A little later we are introduced by St. Luke (10:38-42) to Martha and her sister Mary, who sits at the feet of our dear Lord, much to the chagrin of Martha. This Mary seems quite at ease by Jesus' feet. Then of course there is St. John's account in 20:10-18 of the Mary of Magdala who witnessed Christ's resurrection and was sent to spread the Good News.

According to some, these three women are all of them the woman whom we call Mary Magdalene, though there is no ironclad reason to believe they are actually the same person. The association is due to many things. One of the more interesting is that each of these three women, at some point in Scripture, do a great deal of weeping. This is an odd way to link them, but it is an ancient way. The Old English for Magdalene is Mawdelyn from which we get the English word "maudlin," which refers to one who is overly tearful or sentimental. But let us turn to Mary Magdalene to discover what she has to teach us about liberation.

❧ The Sinful Woman

The first woman, the sinful woman, provides for us a wonderful response to Christ. St. Luke tells us that a woman, a sinner in the city of Nain, comes to Christ out of deep sorrow over sin. She sought him out because she had heard Jesus was in town, in the home of a Pharisee more precisely. Our Lord's reputation had preceded him. Just prior to this scene, he had raised a young man from the dead.

I imagine that, with the kind of interior impulse of love's infinite possibilities, this woman rushed to see the prophet. Perhaps she thought he could heal the dead parts of her which had long since been lost to temptation and sin. Perhaps he could raise her from the slow death of sin. Perhaps he would be willing to just listen and love her for herself.

When she saw him, he was reclined at table. There was no chance for the Pharisee or someone from the Pharisee's household to throw her out, notoriously sinful woman that she was. There was no conversation with anyone, no pleading to be let past some guard. No, she was unstopped as she approached Jesus.

She stood behind Jesus at first, says St. Luke. Then she began to weep. Finally, she collapsed at his feet as the weeping turned into sobbing, the tears streaming over her warm cheeks and falling down upon his feet. She could do nothing but try to dry them with her hair.

Did she have a speech laid out in her mind do you think? Did she plan out what to say to this healing stranger on her way over? Was it even so simple as a phrase like "Teacher, help me."? Whatever she had planned, it was probably not this, not sobbing uncontrollably in public at the feet of a man she had never met before. But there she was. So she opened the jar she carried with her and began to rub the perfumed ointment over Christ's feet.

This Mary Magdalene wept at the feet of Jesus for no other reason but the horror she felt for her own sin, a horror we ought to share. This shows us that the peace of redemption, the sense of release we have when the mill-stone is removed from about our neck, is a liberation much more desirable than any other. Talk of liberation theologies that fail to recognize this lesson have started down a dangerous path. Real change, real revolution and liberation begins in the personal conversion away from sin and not in socio-economic systems.

The Contemplative

Then there is Mary, the Mary of Bethany, who sat at the feet of Jesus. In Luke 10:38-42 Jesus arrives at Bethany and the house of Martha. Martha is busy taking care of all the guests in the house. Our Lord did have quite the entourage. She then complains to Christ, who rebukes her and tells her that Mary has the better part.

In our culture, the one that places so much value in doing and action, there is an instinctive hurt over what Jesus does here. What was poor Martha to do? Here she is slaving away at what was a legitimately important task, and Mary sits there ignoring it all. The people in the pew almost universally feel for Martha, who we think got the short end of the stick. Why should Mary get the better part? Why should hospitality be counted as a second-rate love? Do not passages like this just embolden those who lead pious lives never to lift a finger for the poor?

These are understandable questions, but then do notice please that it is not that Martha asked Jesus his opinion of the situation. She did not plead for mercy. She did not ask, "Could someone help me with all this work?" Nor did she ask, "Lord what would you have me do? What would you have Mary do?" Rather she said, "Lord, do you not care that my sister has left me by myself to do the serving? Tell her to help me." Poor Martha, in a fit of frustration, actually accuses and commands Jesus.

By trying to embarrass her sister in front of everyone, Martha went a bit far and implied that Jesus was somehow deficient in his responsibilities to justice. How could he let Mary sit there, after all? In truth, Martha was accusing Jesus of complicity in Mary's dereliction of duty. She did not suggest an alternative arrangement. She simply told Jesus what he should be doing and why.

Christ's response here is relatively mild considering the affront Martha just leveled at him. He notes that she is anxious, which explains her attitude. "Martha, Martha, you are anxious and troubled about many things." What gentleness we see in Jesus' response. He says her name twice, as a parent would to a child who has disappointed him or her. Jesus reminds her that Mary has chosen the "better part." It is better to sit at the feet of Christ and listen. This is the stance of a "disciple," a word that means student. The disciple is the student sitting, listening, receiving. This is the better part.

Don't we do what Martha did? We are so sure of our own sense of justice that we have no qualms about telling God how to run his business. Whether it is about our own health or career or about the behavior of another, we are quick to make sure we express what should be happening. If we really believed God was in charge, though, we might be better about accepting the present moment.

A long time ago I had the sad experience of speaking with a boy just one year into a Catholic university education. I had known him before he entered college, and in that first year he had gone from the quasi-attentive care of his faith to a total rejection of the Church. He despised the Church. He stated in no uncertain terms that those nuns in the cloister needed to be gotten out of there and put to work for the poor. That, he said, was true social justice.

I have found this attitude at least latent in some social justice literature. Quiet prayer is nice and all, so goes the thinking, but it ought rather be a reflection on action already done, action for the poor. You may keep your Catholic pieties, some say, but they better point to socio-economic change. Jesus' divinity is fine, but the power of his example is the human demand for justice. To this attitude, found as an undercurrent in some social justice teaching, Mary of Bethany gives us a separate lesson.

Mary, sister to Martha, shows us again that liberation theologies are wrong when they insist, above all other things, on doing or "*praxis*," the Greek word for action. Doing is not the foundation of a theology; encounter is, and a true encounter requires receptivity more than activity. *Praxis* is not the start of theology; surrender is. A relationship of surrender to the urging of Christ's loves is the core of discipleship. This is why the example of Mary Magdalene is so important.

Discipleship will and must lead us to action and service. All love is like this. If I claimed to love my wife but *never* bought her flowers or did nice things for her or told her I loved her, she would rightly doubt my love. But the main thing is *not* the service. The flowers and overtures of love are not my love but rather fruits of it. The work of charity and justice must be grounded first in Christ, to whom we should surrender in an encounter of love.

First comes the quiet contemplation on the Word who makes himself available to us in love. Then comes the service, the action, the doing for others that is a requisite piece of the Christian life. Without Christ, though, our service is no different than the philanthropy of Judas, who desired bigger changes.

Judas the Liberator

It is this same Mary of Bethany, the sister of Martha, that Scripture tells us anointed Christ's head and feet in John 12:1-8. This occurs, St. John tells us, immediately after the Pharisees decided to kill Jesus. Knowing this, Jesus stopped his preaching and moved the Apostles to Ephraim. It was there, as he was preparing to go to Jerusalem to die, that Mary anointed him.

The scene is like that of the first with the sinful woman. Christ was at a meal, except he was not surrounded by the prying and suspicious eyes of the Pharisees. Lazarus was there, recently raised from the dead. Martha was, again, serving – dear woman that she is. Mary came behind Jesus and "took a liter of costly perfumed oil made from genuine aromatic nard and anointed the feet of Jesus and dried them with her hair; the house was filled with the fragrance of the oil." (Jn 12:3)

Again we have this woman, like the sinful woman from Nain, anointing Jesus' feet and wiping them with her hair. However, this has a different tone to it. This was not a release of emotion coming from a sense of deep sinfulness. This was a solemn act of loving care. This was a ritual of intense meaning, a foreshadowing of the preparation of Christ's body for burial. The perfume of the oil filled her nostrils and those of the Apostles and Lazarus and Martha, who perhaps stopped what she was doing. They stared and wondered at this care and at the fact that a very expensive jar of ointment had been used in this way.

To this, the Apostles do not react well. According to St. Mark some of them said to themselves indignantly, "'Why has there been this waste of perfumed oil? It could have been sold for more than three hundred days' wages and the money given to the poor.' They were infuriated with her." (Mk 14:4-5)

We hear this complaint in certain circles. There can be justifiable indignation when the Church chooses to spend money on needless edifices

47

instead of helping the needy. When a pastor spends thousands of dollars on granite countertops for the rectory kitchen, there is something sinfully wrong there. But the complaint is also made about build-ing beautiful churches or having golden chalices when those funds could go to the poor.

St. John remembers this incident with the ointment differently than St. Mark. Perhaps there were several of the Apostles angry, but there was one more specifically so. It was Judas Iscariot, he was upset that the expensive nard was used in this way when it could have been given to the poor. St. John tells us that Judas had ulterior motives, but the point is that Judas thought his argument was reasonable and would ring true to the other Apostles.

To Judas the betrayer our dear Lord said, "Leave her alone. Let her keep this for the day of my burial. You always have the poor with you, but you do not always have me." (Jn 12:7-8) People bristle at this line, but it is from Christ's own mouth. And it sets firmly a principle that we ought to use always, namely that the adoration of our God is more important than the socio-economic progress of the world. What profit is there to gain a world free of poverty if we have in the process lost our souls?

That we will always have the poor does not mean that we give up on eradicating poverty where we find it. The point is that the efforts of this life must be connected to Christ or they risk devolving into calculations like those of Judas.

Perhaps this is what made Judas so angry. He was hoping for the great king who would come and transform Palestine, bring about prosperity, right the injustices of the world and create a heaven on earth. He did not want the God-man. He wanted a liberator. He wanted liberation from political plight more than freedom from the shackles of sin, shackles Mary knew only too well. Judas was on a dangerous path.

Jesus' answer here burst that hope in Judas' heart. According to St. Mark, upon getting this rebuke from Christ, Judas left immediately (it's always "immediately" with St. Mark) to find what he could get from the Pharisees for handing Jesus over. Judas was operating under the calculus of the world. If one is not working for "the cause," they must be against "the cause." Judas knew what needed to happen. Jesus must be stopped, because his failure to be the great liberator meant he was distracting the Jews from revolution.

This attitude manifests itself in the Church today. Some argue that unless the Church is working for socio-economic change it is part of the problem of the structures of sin. Progress is what is important, not principle. Power to change the world is the thing. Winning the battle against the "powers that be" is our crusade, and all of it is more important than fidelity to Christ. Change and revolution are more important than whether or not that bread really is the body, blood, soul and divinity of Jesus.

Likewise, so some argue, if only the Church would change its teaching on homosexuality or contraception or the all-male priesthood, then it might be able to enact real social change. One liberation theologian actually argues that, while Christ's divinity is normative of Catholic theology, it is not useful for overturning systems; so we can do without the technicalities of the Nicene Creed. These attitudes and opinions are all too common, and they are not part of the social teaching of the Church any more than they are part of Christ's act of love on the cross.

Mary at the End

In the end, we have Mary Magdalene, specifically named, at the foot of the cross and as the one who first met the Risen Lord.

The love Mary Magdalene has for Christ translates into action in these later chapters of the Gospels. She is the first evangelist. She is to the Apostles the bearer of the good news that Jesus has risen. In St. John's Gospel the scenes are striking in their detail and humanity.

On the morning after the Sabbath, Mary went to the tomb to visit. What was her intention? She could not roll back the stone by herself. Did she just want to be near him? Did the woman who wept at his feet and who sat hanging on every word just want to sit and contemplate those words again in proximity to his corpse? Did she imagine herself sitting with her back to the great stone, perhaps leaning against it just to be close to him once again? When she arrived, though, she found the tomb open.

She dared not enter to discover what happened, so she ran to the Apostles and told them of the situation. Peter and "the other disciple," whom we believe is St. John himself, came out with Mary to go to the tomb. They ran, but Peter was older, so the young John outpaced him. It is a wonderful detail and a more impressive fact that when John arrived before Peter, he did nothing before the older Apostle had arrived. Due reverence was paid to Peter. He was still the leader of the group despite John's fidelity at the foot of the cross and Peter's betrayal. John did peek into the tomb, though, and noticed the linens once around Christ's body were now on the floor. But he did not go in.

When Peter arrived, he entered, leaving Mary and John outside. While the linens are strewn on the floor, Peter noticed that the napkin that had been placed over Christ's face was neatly rolled up and left aside. John then entered and "believes," and the two of them flew back to tell the others.

It was only then that Mary entered the tomb to see what the other two had seen. When she did so there were two angels within asking her why she was weeping. She responds:

"'Because they have taken away my Lord, and I do not know where they have laid him.' When she said this, she turned around and saw Jesus there, but did not know it as Jesus. "Jesus said to her, 'Woman, why are you weeping? Whom are you looking for?' She thought it was the gardener and said to him, 'Sir, if you carried him away, tell me where you laid him, and I will take him.'

"Jesus said to her, 'Mary!' She turned and said to him in Hebrew, 'Rabbouni,' which means Teacher.

"Jesus said to her, 'Stop holding on to me, for I have not yet ascended to the Father. But go to my brothers and tell them, "I am going to my Father and your Father, to my God and your God."

"Mary of Magdala went and announced to the disciples, 'I have seen the Lord,' and what he told her." (Jn 20:13-18)

There is a sweetness about all of this. Mary, still in love with her Lord, wanted only to go be with him. She assumed the strange figure before her was a gardener. She asked about the body so that she might reclaim it, perhaps with the help of the other Apostles. Mary's love will not be hindered no matter the obstacle. Stone or no stone, long distance or none, she will be with Jesus.

But when Jesus said her name, that dread stillness within her began to fill with hope. Her heart like a rose blooming in the darkness was opened, and she said perhaps what she meant to say when she first saw him in the house of the Pharisee so long ago, "Teacher." She grabbed at him. Oh, to embrace the beloved Lord once again! But he was different now. It was not the same.

Her response to Christ's presence, to the return of the man who brought her back to life through casting out her demons, was to go and tell the Good News. Christ was risen from the dead, and he wants to see us again. How was she received by the Apostles? Did it take her long to convince them? Were Peter and John a help or a hindrance? We do not know, but Mary had set one of the first bricks in the edifice of the Church.

At Home with Mary

Tradition tells us that Mary Magdalene accompanied St. John and the Blessed Virgin Mary to the island of Ephesus. That would have been an idyllic life, serving the Mother of God and the beloved disciple.

In the end, we know quite a bit about this Mary. We know of a woman who was healed by Christ. Whether she was the sinful woman of Luke 7 or the woman healed of evil spirits named

Magdalene in Luke 8 does not matter. Both were healed. Who could deny that Mary of Bethany, the contemplative Mary, who longed to sit and listen to Christ, would have kept the ointment and used it to care for the lifeless body of Christ just as Mary Magdalene did. But most important is this story of the sinner turned contemplative turned evangelist. It is one of the greatest of Sacred Scripture. It is markedly instructive for the Christian life.

In her we discover what true liberation is and how much we must foster it through love of Christ, instead of through mere activity. We grow through her story as we increase in understanding about the intimate relationship that discipleship can and ought to be. And we learn that such discipleship cannot be hidden away, but must pour itself out to fill the whole world with the intoxicating aroma of love.

My own father, atheist that he was for the vast majority of his life, would have appreciated St. Mary Magdalene. He knew of the pain of regret and sin. He knew what Christ offered. So in the end he knew he could do nothing else but to reconcile himself with the Church and take Communion for the first time in many decades. Old and frail from cancer, his was a soft conversion of sorts. There was no pursuit of Christ left for him. There was only the furtive hope that he could be healed of his own demons and live fully at the bosom of Abraham. His death on her feast day is a great grace for which I shall be forever grateful.

May St. Mary the sinner, the contemplative, the evangelist intercede for us so that we see what Our Lord offers us, so that we too might come to long only for union with Christ our love, Christ our hope, Christ our King.

Prayer

Dear Mary, teach us to weep for our own sins. Help us trust in Jesus and only in him. Good Mary, help us pursue a life of peaceful rest in Christ. Show us the liberation that we seek. Remind us, when we lose hope and delve into self-hatred, that we are beloved children of God. Teach us to take the better part and listen in quiet admiration to the Lord who is always speaking. Allow us to hear his words, "Go and sin no more," as an invitation to renewed life. Pray that we will take advantage of the Sacrament of Penance and Reconciliation more often and with greater seriousness.

Dear Mary, will you lead us by the hand to the tomb? Will you give us the courage to look in and seek for Jesus? Will you pray that we have the same courage you had to preach the good news?

Mary, help us to serve the Church as you served Our Lady and St. John. Pray to Jesus that we can forever be available to him and to whatever he wills for us. Amen.

Compendium

143. *Freedom mysteriously tends to betray the openness to truth and human goodness, and too often it prefers evil and being selfishly closed off, raising itself to the status of a divinity that creates good and evil: … Human freedom needs therefore to be liberated.* Christ, by the power of his Paschal Mystery, frees man from his

disordered love of self,[13] which is the source of his contempt for his neighbor and of those relationships marked by domination of others. Christ shows us that freedom attains its fulfillment in the gift of self.[14] By his sacrifice on the cross, Jesus places man once more in communion with God and his neighbor.

524. *The Church's social teaching is the indispensable reference point that determines the nature, modality, articulation and development of pastoral activity in the social field.* ... The Church exists and is at work within history. She interacts with the society and culture of her time in order to fulfill her mission of announcing the newness of the Christian message to all people, in the concrete circumstances of their difficulties, struggles and challenges. She does so in such a way that faith enlightens them so that they can understand the truth that "true liberation consists in opening oneself to the love of Christ".[15] ....

IV

THE UNCOMPROMISING
ST. THOMAS MORE

Robert the Bruce, contender for the throne of Scotland, first brings his father news about the rebellion led by William Wallace, a commoner. In the movie "Braveheart," the leprous father instantly devises a plan by which the Bruce clan could simultaneously gain favor with the Scots and the English. The young Robert will support the rebellion in the North while the older man will condemn it in the South. One gets the feeling that Robert is a bit taken aback of this all-too-easy and cold calculation by his father's.

Robert says, "This Wallace. He doesn't even have a knighthood. But he fights with passion, and he inspires." His father replies:

"You admire him this man, this William Wallace. And you wish to charge off and fight as he did, eh? Uncompromising men are easy to admire. He has courage. So does a dog. But it is exactly the ability to compromise that makes a man noble. And understand this, Edward Longshanks is the most ruthless king ever to sit on the throne of England, and none of us, and nothing of Scotland, will remain unless we are as ruthless."

"Uncompromising men are easy to admire." This is perhaps not so much the case today. Much like Robert the Bruce's father, today's world has a habit of admiring the compromising fellow. Thanks to that dictatorship of relativism, the general public is easily offended by anyone who dares stand up for something with uncompromising stolidity.

The defender of objective truths is – so the sages of Manhattan and Melrose Place tell us – no different than the Nazi who insists on the claim to racial purity or the Islamic bomber. Standing on principle, we are told, is for the gauche fundamentalist, the backward dupe in the long lands of corn and wheat somewhere in the middle of the country.

For this reason, the figure of St. Thomas More, whose feast is June 22nd, can be such a perplexing figure for the modern mind. And even the Catholic who consumes his or her breakfast whilst poring over the latest *motu proprio* can miss this astonishingly great man, for it is easy to chalk him up with all the other saints and blesseds who gain God's favor by losing their heads.

If we stop there, though, if we stop just at the fact that he was martyred, we might lose the rest of the story, which is truly the important part. By looking at the rest of the man, we learn that St. Thomas More is more than just a martyr. He is an example of exquisite manhood and parental care, and he can teach us a great deal about the Catholic social teaching we hope to understand and live out.

The Educated Man

Thomas was born on February 6th, 1478 to Sir John More and Agnes Grainger just blocks from St. Paul's Cathedral (Milk Street, Cheapside). He was well born into a wealthy family that could afford to send him to St. Anthony's and then eventually, by the time he was twelve, to Oxford.

Within the early years of his life one discovers an interesting fact. Sir John, Thomas' father, was very strict with his son. While the young More was at Oxford Christchurch there were no bacchanalian romps like those we read about in Evelyn Waugh. Thomas' father saw to that by giving the lad only enough money for necessities.

This is a reminder of the teaching of Blessed Pope John Paul II in *Familiaris consortio* when he speaks to parents about educating their children. He asks parents to be diligent in training the next generation in those matters of essential value. Fascinatingly, the Blessed Holy Father does not tell us that the matters of essential value are particular courses. Rather, they are an attitude. He says that what is essential for the education of youth is to instill in them a proper relationship between their own will and material things. It is important for children to know what a simple life is like. It is, in other words, crucial that children know to appreciate people more than things.

Freedom, we are told by the pope, is not freedom from the State or from stodgy schoolmasters or from bourgeois, patriarchal social structures. What children need is freedom from an *overly active attachment to stuff*. These are stern words to the good people of our time. Even the most well-meaning and faithful of Catholics can spoil their children with stuff. This is an important lesson and one which Sir John followed closely as he raised his son.

Thomas More, because of his lack of time to do much else but study, ends up going to law school in 1496. By 1501 he passed the bar, and in 1504 he became a member of Parliament.

The Spiritual Man

During this time of study, young Thomas fully integrated the hard-won lessons taught by his father. When he was eighteen, he began wearing a hairshirt, a practice he continued until his dying day. He went to daily Mass, a rarity in those days. He prayed all the regular penitential prayers for Fridays and prayed the Little Office. Detachment was part of his regular routine.

Unlike some saints, however, St. Thomas More did not "overdo it." There are countless examples of saints who have to be told by superiors to lighten up on their penances. Some saints learn the hard way that they cannot be so stern towards their bodies. Indeed, St. Francis of Assisi is reported to have said before he died that his one regret was having treated his body, Brother Ass, so harshly. In contrast, Thomas More was ascetical but not loony. Desiderius Erasmus, More's dear friend, once wrote of him "I never saw anyone so indifferent about food…. Otherwise, he has no aversion from what gives harmless pleasure to the body."[16]

Thomas understood – as Blessed John Paul II wrote – that the best education was one which taught you how to have a proper detachment from things. In this was virtue, and Thomas pursued virtue with vigor. He enjoyed life. He enjoyed decent food and wine, but never to excess. He never let it rule him.

Regarding intellectual pleasures, Erasmus and More were close because the two of them loved the Greek and Latin languages. They would "play" at translating Greek sayings into the language of the Church. Their mutual friend William Lily, author of the famous lexicon, was the first man to teach Greek in London. This was the sort of pleasure that young Thomas sought out, a pleasure that required the self-controlled focus of the mind.

St. Thomas More did seriously consider the

priesthood. He was drawn to the Carthusians, the Franciscans and to the diocesan priesthood. He could not, it seems, decide which way God was calling him. This waffling should not be taken as a sign of inconstancy or lack of maturity. It is precisely a sign of great maturity to be open to so many forms of Catholic spirituality: the gorgeous solitude of the Carthusian, the passionate care of the Franciscan, the ever-faithful service of the diocesan priest. These charisms could all be found in Thomas the man, so naturally he was attracted to them all as he discerned how the Lord wished to use him.

This is an important lesson for our time as we try to advise the young men in our lives about discernment. Thomas More was not content to just play at thinking about being a priest. He was not satisfied with the occasional prayer and conversation. Rather, with a sense of purpose he sought out the religious orders and investigated, spending time with each. Only with that information could he possible discern properly. It was then, after having done the work and praying on the information, that he was clear on the call to marriage. It was with that clarity that he pursued his vocation with Jane Colt.

The Family Man

Jane was ten years his junior and the eldest daughter of John Colt of Netherhall, Essex. This is significant because the Colts were not of the nobility or wealthy Londoners. They were the pure and simple folk of the English countryside, the same people that Tolkien, Chesterton, Belloc, Lewis and all of us know to be the steadfast and good folk that inspire characters like the *semper fidelis* Sam Gamgee.

Thomas married Jane after having first been infatuated with Jane's younger sister. William Roper, More's son-in-law, tells us years later that after realizing what an offense it would be for him to pursue the younger sister while the older was unmarried, More "took pity" on Jane and chose her. Roper's version of these events of the heart is perhaps a bit off. By all other accounts, Thomas exemplified yet again his uncompromising desire to do good and avoid evil by taming his desires and bending his will towards the right. "Pity" is not the right word to describe More's attitude towards Jane. Rather, he knew that love is a choice, a firm and determined commitment for the good of the other. It is much more than a mere feeling.

Thomas again shows us that he is not attached to things, to outward appearances or to the conquests of a woman he finds particularly attractive. Feeble infatuation is for the fat-headed. Rather than court the younger sister, he pursued Jane, came to know her, fell in love with her purity and virtue and made that choice to marry her in 1505. Thomas and Jane had four children: Margaret (Meg), Elizabeth, Cecilia and John.

Thomas began right away to tutor his wife, to give her an education better than that which she had received. He carried forth this passion for education to his children, his male and female children. Meg is said to have been a champion classicist. Indeed, by teaching his daughters, Thomas More influenced several of the English nobility into having their girls educated. He believed that girls and boys were equally capable of the demands of a classical education. In this way, he again exemplifies the social teaching of the Church, which makes no distinction between men and women and the right to an education.

Thomas lost his dear wife in 1511. At the time of their mother's death, the children ranged in age from about two to around six. Within months, More married Alice Middleton, a woman seven years his senior, a widow and mother to several children only the youngest of which would join the More household.

The marriage of More and Middleton included a good portion of argument and laughter. Unlike Jane, Dame Alice was not as willing to put up with Thomas' long visits with his learned friends, who would mill about sipping on wine and discussing the intricacies of Greek and Latin grammar. Alice was a practical woman, which is most likely the reason More married her. Still, her impatience was good humored.

He teased her on occasion, and she would complain about his hair shirt. He would try to tell her about the latest scientific theory, and she would berate him for not being ambitious enough. They both would give as good as they got.

Once, in response to a friend's observation about both Jane and Alice being petite women, More said, "If women were necessary evils, was it not wise to choose the smallest evil possible?" On another occasion when writing to a Dutch friend, Dame Alice made her husband write:

> "My wife bids me give you a thousand greet-ings, and thanks you for your very careful salutation, in which you wished her a long life, of which she says she is all the more desirous, that she may plague me the longer."[17]

Humor was a good part of the More house-hold as was religious piety. Every evening, the entire house gathered for prayers including servants, cooks, stable men and boys, friends and visitors. During dinner, a passage and commentary on Scripture would be read by one of the children while everyone listened. After that was done, talk about their days would ensue.

Nobles were rarely, if ever, invited to dinner and the wealthy only occasionally. More's brighter friends, those lovers of Greek and Latin like Erasmus, would visit and spend long nights. But More was also in the habit of going out into the village to invite the poor to come and sup. He took seriously the words of Christ, "Rather, when you hold a banquet, invite the poor, the crippled, the lame, the blind." (Lk 14:13) St. Thomas knew that injustice was not having more than his neighbor. The injustice was in not sharing it with those who truly needed it.

Good Thomas More was also known for insisting that he be told whenever a woman from the village was going into labor. When informed, he would pray for her, throughout the night if necessary, until he was told about the outcome. Good or ill, he would often take the time to travel to the home in order to greet the family and offer his help.

This is not the stuff of an out-of-touch sap-of-a-saint who, with rosy cheeks, appears on our saint cards awash in light and glitter. This was a man who lived life to serve and to do so in the Spirit of the Savior. This was a man of virtue who sought to carefully fulfill his obligations to his family and neighbors. In short, St. Thomas More was a righteous man before he ever ran up against the intemperate nature of Harry, king of England.

The Vicious Man, Henry

King Henry VIII had been crowned the King of England in 1509 at the ripe old age of eighteen. Remember that at the same age More was wearing hairshirts and attending daily Mass, King Harry was instead debauching young lasses as best he could.

In the age of arranged marriages, it was proposed by Spain – the seat of the Holy Roman Empire – and by England and Rome that Catherine of Aragon, the daughter of the famed Ferdinand and Isabella, marry Harry's brother Arthur, the Prince of Wales and heir to the throne. Unfortunately for Catherine, the marriage ended quickly. She and Arthur became ill very shortly after being married in November of 1501. She survived but he died in April the next year. The marriage, Catherine claimed, was never consummated.

This was an important fact. According to the Church's canon law, a man could not marry his brother's widow. There was also the question of the dowry which ought to have been returned to Spain. Thus it was that a dispensation was sought from the pope; the marriage with Arthur was deemed never consummated; and it was decided that Henry would marry Catherine, about whom he had grown quite obsessed. She was said to be a stunningly lovely woman. They married in 1509 after some political delays and enjoyed several pregnancies with only one surviving child, Mary.

What follows is the sad history of the betrayals of King Henry against poor Catherine. Protestant or Catholic, nearly everyone recognizes that Catherine of Aragon was treated most dreadfully by Henry. After siring an illegitimate son with one woman, the king took up with a young thing, a married woman named Mary Boleyn. Henry, though, grew tired of her and so pursued her sister

Anne Boleyn.

It was finally Anne who pressed Henry to get rid of Catherine, perhaps more out of a sense of self-preservation than malice towards Catherine. It was later that the Boleyn family chaplain, Thomas Cranmer, was made the Archbishop of Canterbury in order to illicitly nullify the marriage between Catherine and the King. It was the Boleyn family friend Thomas Cromwell who prosecuted St. Thomas More and proceeded, with Cranmer and King Harry, to sack every Catholic monastery in England. Indeed, it could very well be said that it was the Boleyn family that brought down the Catholic Church in England, and all of it because of the tempestuous and inconstant nature of King Henry VIII.

The Uncompromising Man

In contrast, then, we have Thomas More, who had become Lord High Chancellor of England in 1529. The previous Chancellor was Cardinal Wolsey, who was at the same time Chancellor and one of the leading clerics of England. Wolsey had failed to secure the annulment from Catherine that King Harry wanted and so was tossed aside. More knew he could not last long as the Chancellor if he did not support the annulment with Catherine, and he didn't. Thus, he resigned his post in 1532. The virtuous More, when put to the test, decided to place his family's fortune at risk rather than to violate his conscience against the truth.

We may have had the experience of a little voice in the mind that pops up to say, "It's only a little lie," or "Who will know?" or "Don't quit, stay part of the system so that you can change it for the good." No, More understood that the power he wielded as Chancellor would corrupt. Absolute power corrupts absolutely Lord Acton would say years later. Good intentions do not unmake the damage done by twisted consciences. So, to thwart the will of the Church in the name of Harry's vice was to claim for himself a power he knew could only corrupt him. He wisely avoided the issue and resigned as Chancellor.

For the next year and a half, the More family learned to live rather frugally. Thomas engaged in writing some tracts against this or that heresy and about matters of law but did not comment on the situation with that Boleyn girl and the King. He refused to attend the coronation of Anne , and so his absence and silence began to be a problem.

In 1533, when Boleyn and the King were married by Cranmer, the Holy Father excommunicated them all. In 1534 the King introduced to Parliament the Act of Succession which required all to recognize Anne as the rightful Queen and her offspring, namely Elizabeth, as the rightful heir. To refuse to accept this decree was to admit to treason.

Thomas More, widely respected figure that he was, was asked to comment on the Act. He gave none. He was asked again and pressed to make some statement. Again he gave none, but the meaning was plain to everyone. Thomas More did not accept the decree. He was then put under house arrest, carted off to some holding area and sent to the Tower of London, where he spent the next fifteen months.

The imprisoned More has not denied or admitted to anything. He simply refused to give an opinion on the matter. But King Henry knew this was not good enough. He needed More on his side. He needed More to speak publicly in favor of the Act. Cromwell knew the same. Such is the power of a virtuous man. Even his silence is deafening.

Dame Alice, Margaret, her husband William Roper and other friends attempted to persuade Thomas against his silence. Compromise! You can almost hear the leper father of Robert the Bruce saying it, "It is exactly the ability to compromise that makes a man noble."

Our world, the world of the politically savvy, would tell us that it takes a noble man to compromise, to recognize when he's beat and to move on for the greater good. But More would not compromise, not when it came to *fundamental* truths of the faith and of the sanctity of marriage, not when it came to the meaning of an oath. For the sake of truth he could not compromise any more than he could deny the existence of his own right hand or the beauty in his children's eyes.

While in prison, More wrote this:

"Give me, good Lord, a longing to be with thee: not for the avoiding of the calamities of this wicked world, nor so much for the avoiding of the pains of Purgatory, nor of the pains of Hell neither, nor so much for the attaining of the joys of Heaven in respect of mine own commodity, as even for a very love of thee."[18]

We can almost hear More's internal struggle. Does he maintain his position for pride's sake? Is he merely avoiding the pains of this world? Is he engaging in a kind of political protest with his life? Or is he banking on going to heaven, presumptuous and so, again, prideful? This is why More prays that his act of conscience come not from any of these but from the love of Christ, from an urgency that is the fruit of his love of God. So many of us involved in social justice work need this sort of conscientious discernment. This is what Catholic social teaching is calling for: not political protest but sincere movements of the heart filled with love of God.

Consider, too, More's language. The imprisoned man still prays to the "good Lord." Despite the turn of fortune in life and the lives of many of his loved ones, he still prays with the words "good Lord." Do we accept such suffering and persecution with equal grace?

The charge was treason against the King, and the trial was a sham, a lurid show of despicable greed and corruption. The injustices were heaped one upon another. Yet, Thomas sat at peace. He defended himself, but he was at peace.

On July 6th, 1535, good Thomas More, noble Thomas More, is taken to the scaffold to die. When the time came, he walked up the steps of the scaffold and exchanged a joke with the guard. He greeted the executioner and wished him well, encouraging him in his duty. He prayed the *Miserere* with fervor and announced to all that he was dying for the Catholic Faith and declared himself, "The King's good servant – but God's first." He then peaceably placed his head on the block but asked for a moment to move his beard, since, he said, it had committed no treason. He was fifty-seven years old.

Marriage and Family

This family man, this political figure, this lawyer, this saint shows us that losing one's head is not what makes us close to God. Getting oneself killed for Jesus is not the lesson to be learned here. Rather it is the attitude towards this world, an attitude that is simultaneously detached from things while being attached to the service of persons for the sake of Christ.

For these reasons, St. Thomas More is a marvelous example of what Catholic social teaching is all about. He understood that the political life is not the end-all-be-all for the human person. Politics are for people not people for politics. Having it the other way around usually crushes the human conscience into bits. When politics are the most important thing, when power is the prize, a politician's mind and heart are usually made deaf to the cries of his own conscience, which pleads for justice and righteousness. So the focus has to be on people, on the truth and on fidelity to principle.

The full life, More understood, is lived through a conscience in tune with the will of God. A vibrant society makes room for the pursuit of the divine and the adventure of orthodoxy so wonderfully described by the likes of G.K. Chesterton. But such a society is only possible if truth is granted its due. About truth we must be uncompromising. The moment we have given up on truth, we have sacrificed our hope for social justice.

St. Thomas also shows us that love in truth is founded first in the family. From his own father to the way he parented his children, More showed himself as a prime example of what Blessed John Paul II states in *Familiaris consortio*. The family is the first school of the social teaching. In the family, children learn what self-giving love is. In the family, children first understand what service for the other can do for the soul. Thus, the family becomes not just a building block for society, a kind of cog in a wheel of the machine. Rather, the family is a society unto itself. Family is the thing upon which the rest of society must be modeled. Woe to those who pass laws to undermine the family.

The law of self-giving love in the family is

founded on marriage. So when marriage is torn asunder, when the truth of marriage is traded in for a ruse, then the law of love is harder to see and social justice is that much harder to achieve. St. Thomas More was a man who practiced the law of self-giving throughout his life because of his experience of family and because of his dedication to the sanctity of marriage.

Therefore, care for the defense of marriage cannot be a position compromised for the sake of a false nobility. Tolerance for its own sake is a meager shadow of what is truly noble. Though we may not have the articulation for it, we ought to stand firm on the nature of marriage. Though we are and will continue to be persecuted for it, we must live and serve authentic marital love. Though our political class may not be willing to hear it, we must defend traditional marriage in the law. This too is a social justice issue.

The contemporary Catholic who defends marriage will come off as brutish and closed to the modern man. And certainly there are imprudent ways of articulating the Church's teaching. But then, St. Thomas More shows us that to be uncompromising for the truth is to live in the righteousness of the God who loves. Love should always be the measure, and it is not the stagnant love that demands freedom to redefine marriage and do away with the Gospel. Real love is that which fulfills the vows in their entirety. Real love exists with the gift of the whole self.

St. Thomas More, defender of religious liberty and man of conscience, pray for us so that we might learn to be as prudently uncompromising as you, reminding us always to serve our true sovereign, Christ the King.

Prayer

Dear Thomas, we are often overwhelmed with opportunities to compromise our faith. Help us to have peace. Pray that we have the prudence necessary to know when to speak, what to say and when to stop talking.

Help us as well with our children, dear Thomas. Despite our prayers and examples, we are not always successful at inspiring in them a lasting faith. Knowing yourself what it is to be a parent, intercede for us. Help us know how to reach them. Help us pass on the faith to them in a way that will take hold so that they don't throw it aside at the first opportunity.

Good Thomas, pray to Jesus that we are better about following his will instead of our own. And pray that, when faced by intrusions of the government against our faith, pray that we have the courage you had to stand up for the faith and defend the truth. Amen.

Compendium

399. … Unjust laws pose dramatic problems of conscience for morally upright people: *when they are called to cooperate in morally evil acts they must refuse.*[19] Besides being a moral duty, such a refusal is also a basic human right which, precisely as such, civil law itself is obliged to recognize and protect. …

It is a grave duty of conscience not to cooperate, not even formally, in practices which, although permitted by civil legislation, are contrary to the Law of God. Such cooperation in fact can never be justified, not by invoking respect for the freedom of others nor by appealing to the fact that it is foreseen and required by civil law. No one can escape the moral responsibility for actions taken, and all will be judged by God himself based on this responsibility (cf. *Rom* 2:6; 14:12).

553. *Promoting human dignity implies above all affirming the inviolability of the right to life, from conception to natural death,* the first among all rights and the condition for all other rights of the person.[20] Respect for personal dignity requires, moreover, that *the religious dimension of the person be recognized.* "This is not simply a requirement 'concerning matters of faith', but a requirement that finds itself inextricably bound up with the very reality of the individual".[21] The effective recognition of the *right to freedom of conscience and religious freedom* is one of the highest goods and one of the most serious duties of every people that truly wishes to ensure the good of the individual and of society.[22] In the present cultural context, there is a particularly urgent need to *defend marriage and the family,* which can be adequately met only if one is convinced of the unique and singular value of these two realities for an authentic development of human society.[23]

V

THE SELFLESS HEART OF
ST. JOAN DELANOUE

In the middle of August every year, the Church remembers a unique woman. She was a business
woman who, out of love for the poor, gave up her
work. Her love for them was a result of something
that was part mystical experience and part
encounter with a crazy, old beggar woman who
spoke to God. Her conversion was thanks to a
priest who was the only one she could find that
neither bored her to tears nor tried to ruin her. This
woman celebrated on August 17th is Saint Joan
Delanoue, or St. Joan of the Cross, and she has a lot
to teach us.

By the Book

St. Joan was born the youngest of twelve
children in 1666 in Saumur, France, about 50 miles

West of Tours. Her parents, besides loving their many children, were shopkeepers who sold drapes, crockery and those ubiquitous trinkets that appear around Catholic shrines. In Saumur, it was a shrine dedicated to Notre Dame of Ardilliers, sometimes called Our Lady of Pity, as the image is of Mary with Christ's lifeless body draped across her lap.

Joan grew up Catholic in Catholic France, but the faith did not enthuse her. Droning curates recited the lessons at Mass again and again, and joy seemed to be lacking in those local priests. Her mind wandered, as would anyone's, and so the faith was not a personal anything. There was no Christ to get to know, there were only the lessons to be learned, the rules to be followed.

In such a parish, the heart atrophies. Doing the will of Christ becomes only a matter of checking boxes and completing one's duty. The great mission of Jesus to love God with total commitment and one's neighbor as oneself is summed up through mundane encouragements towards obligation. Many know how impossible heroism becomes when love is defined by so meager a measure as obligation. It was the same with Joan.

Nevertheless, Joan followed these rules very well, perhaps too well. She may have suffered from scrupulosity, that spiritual ailment where the person is convinced that every thought and action must be sinful. Whatever the case, Joan never learned to take those rules to mean anything more than what they were. She did not know to look beyond them or more deeply into them. The rules were the rules. She could not see them as pointers to a loving God, for she did not know this God. As a result, the rules were plastic things which must not be ignored but rather made to suit one's need when necessary. In this way, Joan maintained the illusion of following the rules and getting her own way too.

Bending the rules was of course often necessary, because on top of it all, as the youngest of twelve children to two working parents, Joan was lost in the hustle and bustle of life. Her natural selfishness was left unchecked. Rules, always meant to serve her interests, would be interpreted in a manner that best fit her needs. Catholicism for Joan, if one can call it that at the beginning, was no faith at all. It was a game. That was seemingly the only way to make it interesting.

The Business Woman

When she was twenty-five years old, with the death of her parents, Joan inherited the house and the shop they ran. She went into partnership with her seventeen-year-old niece who shared the same name, the same looks and the same interest in making money.

The first thing these young women of moxy did was to start selling goods on Sundays and Feast Days. These are the days when pilgrims are nearest a shrine after all. Why not open the back door of the gift shop and sell a little something here and there? What would be the harm? Oh, how the profiteering mind works!

Normally, that is when Joan's parents ran the place, more profits meant more money to give to the poor, but this was another change about the shop. While the late Mrs. Delanoue would give to beggars at the door, young Mademoiselle Delanoue did not. "I have nothing to give you," was her response to the hungry person come begging. While this was true, Joan often did not have anything *to give them*, it was because Joan was playing with the rules.

You see, Joan and her niece were very frugal, counting every penny, and so routinely made decisions about purchases in order to help them "honestly" deny the poor at the door. For instance, Joan never kept any food in the house. Just before they were to sit down to eat, she would send her niece to the alimentary for some food. When a beggar came to the door, Joan would "honestly" say that there was no food to share. There would be no money to give them either, because Joan and her niece had adroitly spent it on the finest of dresses, and what good is a dress to a beggar?

These two young women became rather inventively callous. They were both aware and accepted the obligation, the rule, given by Christ to share with those in need. They just made sure, in a kind of twisted moral calculus, that they were never in a position to be able to share with those in need when asked. This is sadly a frequent, human activity that manifests itself in many ways.

How often, after all, do we "follow the rules" in order to keep what we have, to protect our own bit of comfort and property? Or have we ever embraced one obligation we enjoy in order to get out of another we do not? It goes something like this: I had better start fixing the lawn mower so that I can't be bothered with helping around the house. That too is a game.

Or how often do we pour over our budget saying there is not enough money for the tithe, but there is enough for dining out or for the gadget with the extra buttons? How is it that we have enough for the cable TV that brings an awful lot of filth into the home – along with fascinating documentaries on World War II amphibious vehicles – but not enough for the Church's collection for the retired religious? Joan Delanoue was much like we are today.

This dear, young, ambitious woman of the world was lost in her own avarice and yet was at least somewhat convinced of her own moral righteousness. Keep in mind she was still attending Mass. She was still following the rules of the faith, for the most part. Yes, she sold goods on Sunday, but then the pilgrims chose to buy them. She was just providing a service, that's all. We all play those games. And so poor, lost Joan just plodded along to the tune of her own change-purse. That is until one of God's little jesters traipsed into her life.

The Jester

On the eve of the Epiphany, the feast where the Christ child is presented to the world through three wise men, the childlike visage of Madame Frances Souchet appeared in the town of Saumur. The people of the area could not say whether this woman of Rennes was mentally disabled, just slightly slow in her thinking or an actual prophet of God. Whatever the case, this beggar woman would flit from shrine to country shrine visiting the faithful of those towns and spreading her message. She had the habit of telling people precisely what God was telling her.

Joan allowed Souchet to stay in her home during her latest visit. Joan couldn't deny, after all, that there was a home to share. However, Souchet unnerved Joan with babble about God sending her to Joan's home and about there being a word for her from God. The woman's speech was a series of nonsensical statements strung together, but Souchet seemed so sincere about what she had to say that Joan had to admit that there was a touch of the otherworldly about this lady. Even after she left town, Joan kept mulling over the things the old woman had said. "God sent me this first time to learn the way."[24] *Learn the way*? Joan thought. *To where? To what? And this is just the "first time"? What if God is really talking to me through this madwoman*?

Joan, so disturbed by Souchet, started to seek spiritual balm like she had never done before. So, she took special care to listen to the sermons of the local pastors instead of just tuning them out. She found, however, that they were still droning on, still delivering the stale recitations of this or that Scripture verse. For Joan, this would not do. Her spirit now needed a bit more.

During Lent she resolved to travel further out of town in order to hear different pastors, anyone who could help her understand what was disturbing her peace. Eventually she found Fr. Geneteau, who was the chaplain at the state-run hospital. It was Fr. Geneteau who told her that one of the first things she could do to find peace was to stop selling goods on Sundays and Feast Days. She stopped. She also took up fasting. Then things got interesting.

On Pentecost of 1693, Madame Souchet, the odd beggar-oracle of God, finished her rounds to the neighboring shrines and was back in Saumur. She immediately sought out Joan. In her monologue to Joan there was a lot of "He said this..." and "He said that...," but the gist of it was that God had a plan for Joan, one which he had hatched in his infinite mind and was now communicating to her through this old woman.

Joan began to believe. She came to understand from Souchet that God wanted her to serve the poor and that she would be judged in the end on her care of the poor. There is something in Scripture about that after all, about feeding the hungry, giving drink to the thirsty. Joan could certainly recall this Scriptural injunction along with the story of the rich young man, and so she began to divest herself of her earthly goods. The first thing to go was a glorious dress.

It is remarkable what changes can come over a person when they realize that God is not merely a spectator and that Jesus is not just an historical figure we ought to admire. Joan's openness to change came when she realize that Christ wanted a personal relationship with her, that God cared what she did with her life. Christ Jesus was all of a sudden alive for Joan, and the task of discovering his will was now her most important mission.

Providence House

About two weeks later, the shift in Joan's outlook on life was confirmed in a vision. One morning, quite unexpectedly, the niece found Joan in ecstasy. It lasted three days and nights. What Joan received was a clear call that she was to serve the poor, that she would have others join her, that Fr. Geneteau would be her director and that Our Lady would be her guide. A problem for Joan remained, however: what poor, which poor and where were they?

Souchet provided Joan with an answer. The prophetess said, "He told me that you are to go to Saint-Florent and look after six poor children in a stable there." Sometimes the Lord can be so wonderfully specific. Still, Saint-Florent-des-Bois was some 91 miles southwest of Saumur. It was not a hop, skip or a jump. Despite this, Joan went.

To her great surprise, there in the town was a stable, and there in the stable were six children and their parents starving. Using her own money to buy supplies, Joan cared for them immediately. She personally nursed them back to health. Upon returning to Saumur, she began to take in the beggars at the door, especially the lost children. By 1698, five years after her conversation with Souchet, Joan had taken in so many that she could not care for them all and keep the shop open at the same time. She chose Christ and closed the shop.

After a time, Joan and her niece became guardians of a dozen orphans in their small ancestral house built near a cliff. The townsfolk called it "Providence House" because no one knew how this woman, with no income, was caring for the children. Madame Souchet would say, "The King of France won't give you his purse; but the King of Kings will always keep his open for you."[25]

Not everyone in the town was approving. It is an old tactic of the evil one to prick the hearts of men and women with enough jealousy, pride and self-righteousness so as to look down upon someone doing honest, loving work. Such was the case within Saumur. Several townspeople were convinced it was all doomed to failure, and they openly scoffed at her. They were almost proved right when the cliff behind the house gave way and part of the house collapsed, killing one of the children.

For a time, the Oratorian fathers gave her their stable to stay in, but then they kicked her out because of the steady stream of a "bad element" that came to their doors. Let us pause there for a moment. The priests kicked her out of their stables because the poor she served disturbed their peace. With these sorts of examples of the priesthood, we can forgive our little Joan a bit for not having been too zealous about the faith until now. For the next three years, she lived in whatever cramped quarters she could find, all the while continuing to serve the poor that came to her.

During this three-year period Joan and her niece were joined by Joan Bruneau and Anne Mary Tenneguin. In 1704, with the approving advice of Fr. Geneteau, they began to wear religious garb, calling themselves the Sisters of St. Anne of Providence.

In 1706, discouraged by the numbers of the poor she had to turn away because of lack of space, Joan applied her moxy to the gruff Oratorians who had earlier kicked her out. If they wouldn't give her their stable, she asked, would they lease to her their great-house. The Oratorians agreed, and promptly raised the rent 150%. Oh, how the profiteering mind works!

It was also in 1706 that St. Louis Marie Grignion de Montfort visited Saumur. St. Louis, many may know, is the father of the definitive consecration to Our Lady, known as the *Total*

Consecration to Jesus Through Mary, and the author of *True Devotion to Mary*. He had come to pray at the shrine of Notre Dame de Arilliers in order to ask Our Lady for blessings for the religious communities he was about to found. Though at first harsh with Joan for all her many mortifications, St. Louis Marie eventually said to her, "Go on in the way you have begun. God's spirit is with you; it is He who is leading you in this penitential way. Follow His voice, and fear no more."[26]

The next ten years were filled with ups and down. The sisters were officially recognized as an order and so could take vows. Joan took the religious name of Joan of the Cross, and what a cross she bore. The Oratorians criticized Joan for taking communion every day. They considered this unseemly because, in the Jansenist attitudes of the clergy of the time, no one could be *that* holy. Yes, the priests who had kicked her out because of her care for the poor, the same ones who were engaged in price gouging, thought themselves holy enough to judge her state of soul. But just as things were looking their worst, the Providence of God won out.

A Mr. Henry de Vallière became the Sisters' benefactor, and he attracted more patrons. By 1717 Sr. Joan had moved from the little Providence House that once was her home to the Great Providence House that would be the foundation of her work for the poor. By 1721, Sr. Joan and her companions began to expand their work.

St. Joan of the Cross Delanoue led the community for many more years, ever reminding her sisters about trust in God's Providence, about embracing the Cross of Christ Jesus and about the call to love the poorest of the poor. On August 17th, 1736, Joan left this life and went to meet her beloved Jesus.

Discernment is a Habit

This saintly life is so interesting because there was no unseemly, sensual sin that marred this woman before her conversion. It was not as though she was a drunkard or a prostitute. She was in fact quite fastidious about following the rules of her faith. Dutiful and exacting in her moral rationalizations, Joan would easily fit within our own parishes today.

Sadly, like so many today, she associated faith in Christ Jesus with dutiful behavior and nothing more. Her sins may have been many, but they were understandable, were that not? Beautiful things are good, after all. The danger is that things can consume and enslave us. The soul must be ever mindful of that. Joan would ultimately embrace the Cross in order to find true freedom from that type of enslavement.

Another lesson from St. Joan of the Cross is that she was willing to listen to the unlikeliest of voices when discerning God's call. We ought to ask ourselves to whom are we listening. Are we potentially drowning out the voice of the Lord in our lives with the overbearing blather of talking heads? Do we distract our hearts by the activity with which we fill our lives? Do we dismiss out of hand the words of someone because we think they pray too much to be normal or because they smell bad?

What about those who God gave to help us on the path to heaven: our spouse, our pastor, our parents or even our children? Have we ignored their contribution to our discernment? Once we hear God's voice, do we act upon it, or do we pretend not to have heard? Worse, do we perform the littlest part necessary? Do we behave as though we are throwing God a bone by going through the motions of following his will?

If we are ever to live the social teaching of the Church, then we need to be attentive to the voice of God. Once attentive, we need to carry out the Lord's wish as any young lover would when given a task by his or her beloved. Not only would we do it, we would do it promptly and with joy. We would strive to exceed our love's expectations and present the final product as a gift, not as a burden unloaded. In short, the central lesson of the social teaching is that we must work for others as people in love with Christ Jesus, for Jesus' love must be the purpose and the cause of our action.

To live this way, then, we ought to notice that St. Joan reformed the little transgressions in her life before she answered the heroic call of selling everything. Not all have her vocation. But like St.

Joan we must all look at the little transgressions in which we engage, the rules that we bend and break in order to make our lives easier. We need to guard our eyes and ears from those destructive lessons of the world, so that in hearing God's will we may begin to build the habit of acting on it. In this way the Gospel can penetrate our whole lives.

Wherever we find ourselves in the spiritual life, hopefully Saint Joan can help us discern God's will. We pray that St. Joan of the Cross can help show us where we need reform. St. Joan, pray for us, and long live Christ the King.

Prayer

Dear Joan, though we might follow all the disciplines of the Church and adhere to the Church's teaching, at times we may feel empty in our faith. Pray that we can find that spiritual director or confidant who can help us know Christ as closely as you did. Pray that we have your hope and trust. Pray too that we are able to hear all those in our lives right now who are calling us into deeper relationship with Jesus.

Good Joan, pray to the Father that we can hear his call and then follow it with trust in his plan. Help assuage our constant worry about our bills and other financial concerns. Pray that we find the discipline necessary to live within our means, but at the same time to be generous to those who are in greater need than us.

Joan, teach us that wonderful mystery by which we receive more the more we give away. Amen.

Compendium

285. *Sunday is a day that should be made holy by charitable activity, devoting time to family and relatives, as well as to the sick, the infirm and the elderly. ... Moreover, Sunday is an appropriate time for the reflection, silence, study and meditation that foster the growth of the interior Christian life. Believers should distinguish themselves on this day too by their*

moderation, avoiding the excesses and certainly the violence that mass entertainment sometimes occasions.[27]

540. *This pastoral work in the social sector also includes the work of consecrated persons according to their particular charism. Their shining witness, especially in situations of great poverty, represents a reminder to all people of the values of holiness and generous service to one's neighbor.* The total gift of self-made by men and women religious is offered to the contemplation of everyone as an eloquent and prophetic sign of the Church's social doctrine. Placing themselves totally at the service of the mystery of Christ's love for mankind and the world, religious anticipate and show by their very lives some of the traits of the new humanity that this social doctrine seeks to encourage. In chastity, poverty and obedience, consecrated persons place themselves at the service of pastoral charity, especially by prayer, thanks to which they contemplate God's plan for the world and beg the Lord to open the heart of all persons to welcome within themselves the gift of a new humanity, the price of Christ's sacrifice.

VI

GRACE AND MERCY,
ST. MARIA GORETTI

If you find yourself in Rome, walk over to the Church of John and Paul, Giovanni e Paolo, along the Clivo di Scauro. Across the diminutive piazza in front of the church is a Passionist monastery with an incline leading up to the front door. If you knock at that door, you will, perhaps, be greeted by a fellow in plain clothes.

In either broken Italian or English you can ask to see Maria Goretti, and, without much fanfare, the fellow will probably let you in and lead you to an office. He will open a door to a curio that covers an entire wall of the office, and you will notice in that curio different religious symbols, pieces of paper and some sacred items. Your guide will reach out with surety and grab what appears to be a paper pouch, one of several lined up on their ends in a box.

The fellow, a bit excited now, will hand you the pouch, a piece of parchment paper folded in on itself and hiding within a small relic. He will unfold it for you and point with a smile saying "Santa Maria Goretti."

The Passionists love Maria Goretti because it was under their instruction that she received her First Communion. Since then, they have taken her as one of their own, and rightly so. In the midst of the various passions which women, young women in particular, have to suffer in this day and age, St. Maria Goretti is one of those saints that can stand before us as a great sign of the redemptive value of suffering, of a cleansing passion. We celebrate her every July 6th, for she is the quintessentially un-modern girl who stood up for chastity, modesty and religion. She did it all by saying "yes" to Christ and "no" to the world.

Strength in Adversity

Maria Goretti, affectionately called Marietta by her family, was born in Corinaldo in 1890 on the Eastern side of Italy, just some thirty miles from Ancona. She was the eldest of five children of Luigi and Assunta Goretti. In 1896 the family began to move around a bit, finally settling on the opposite side of Italy in Ferriere near the port town of Nettuno, which sits in the shadow of great Rome.

If one has studied the history of Rome, one knows that the earliest attempts to domesticate the seven hills required draining the swamps. The Cloaca Maxima, or "great sewer," was built in 600 B.C. and channels the water from the swamps into the Tiber River. Over the years, especially during times of Medieval neglect, the swamp water would come back and with it malaria. That disease was rampant in Rome and all along the Roman *campagna* when the Goretti family moved there. So it was that Luigi, after a year of back-breaking work, contracted the disease and died ten days later. Poor Assunta had her five children to raise in the new and strange town of Ferriere. Thankfully, she had Maria to help her.

Though a good deal of her life before her martyrdom is seemingly veiled – we normally only hear about the end – there is actually a great deal to note. Maria Goretti was afraid that her father's soul would remain in Purgatory for too long, so she prayed constantly. This habit of prayer led to long, practiced meditation on the Paschal Mystery, Christ's suffering and death. The rosary was constantly tied around her wrist since, after a time, she could not go long without praying it.

Maria was a diligent daughter who cared for her mother and helped with the other children. With their father gone, it was up to Assunta to work the fields. Maria, only nine years old, cooked and cleaned as a mother would. When there was work to do, she would not go and play, but would rather stick to the chores of the home. We also know that this was not done begrudgingly but rather in a spirit of joyful love for Jesus. And we know that it was from Assunta that Maria learned never to sin "at any cost."

She was a girl of strong will. When she reached the age for First Communion, Maria insisted on receiving despite the many obstacles in her way. Her mother argued that there was no time for preparation, no money to pay for the proper dress and veil and no way that Maria could read or write well enough to learn her catechism. Undaunted, Maria found a way and received First Communion in May 1902 just a few weeks before her martyrdom. The whole town pitched in to get her the proper attire. Before ever a drop of blood was spilled by this devout virgin, she was known for her piety, her modesty and her grandly attractive purity.

The Lost Boy

Now, when the Goretti family had first moved to Ferriere, Luigi Goretti, Maria's father, had partnered with Giovanni Serenelli for sharecropping labor. Serenelli had a son Alessandro and with him lived next to the Goretti's in separate apartments but with a shared kitchen. Luigi Goretti was soon to regret this partnership with Giovanni Serenelli. He was a drinker and prone to loud and immodest language. On his deathbed, Luigi begged his wife to return to Corinaldo. Their debt prohibited the return trip. Thus, when Luigi died, the

Serenellis were quickly an added yoke to the lives of Assunta and Maria Goretti.

Alessandro Serenelli was like the typically despondent, teenage male of our own time. His mother had died in a psychiatric hospital while he was young. Following his father's footsteps, he drank. He had at one time practiced the Catholic faith that fills the air and is dug deep into the sands of Italy. However, bad books and pornography contaminated his mind. He put up pictures of scantily clad women in his room, grew to despise all things religious and, like the petulant boy who cannot stand to see beauty without owning it, he began to proposition Maria.

She was only eleven years old, but her physical and moral beauty, and of course her proximity, made her more than Alessandro's twisted soul could resist. Offers for favors were followed by lewd comments. Comments were followed by assurances that he would have her. Assurances were followed by demands which were followed by threats. With each escalation Alessandro grew bitterer towards the girl who resisted him. Was she too good for him? Was she making fun of him behind his back? Wouldn't she just give in if he applied enough force?

Though Maria did beg her mother not to leave her alone with Alessandro, she did not tell anyone of these advances and the inappropriate behavior. For one thing, even if they were true, who would defend her honor? Her father was dead. Also, who would repair the damage done between the Goretti and the Serenelli families after such an accusation? They were neighbors, indeed partners, and in those days that meant that you depended on each other. Her family was in a precarious state as it was. There is little reason to believe that the very nearly alcoholic Giovanni Serenelli would have done anything anyway.

Fortitude

On a hot July 5th in 1902 Maria was sitting inside her home at the top of the stairs mending a shirt. Alessandro, who was eighteen years old, arrived and bounded up those same stairs. He called her into the shared kitchen of the house with obvious intentions. He had done this before, and Maria had always refused. However, this time Alessandro did not give her a choice. He grabbed her and tossed the girl into the room. There were others in the house, but Alessandro did not care. His was a force of determined lust.

Holding her by the neck he demanded she give in to him. She could only gasp, but with those gasps she said, "No! No! It is a sin!"

The sin to which St. Maria Goretti refers is not to suggest that she would have sinned if Alessandro had forcefully taken her. In that case she would have borne no responsibility and would not have sinned at all. But Alessandro did not wish to physically force himself on her. He sought to convince her to say "yes" to him through the threat of violence. It was her "yes" that he wanted. She would not give it to him. She would not cooperate with his sin in any way.

In this moment, this girl two months short of her twelfth birthday was concerned with her immortal soul and his. This sort of uncompromising stand against cooperation with evil is impressive in anyone, much less this girl so young. There are men of many years with comfortable lives and in charge of a good deal of money who are not so stalwart in their ethical dealings, even when they have far less to lose than poor Maria.

Her response drove Alessandro mad. She did not just say "no"; she said "never." If not him, he thought, then no one. He tore her dress and began stabbing. There was no reason in the violence. He stabbed her fourteen times, the last time leaving the dagger in her back. This was furious anger, unbridled rage and all-consuming lust all in one moment. Then Alessandro ran away. The little boy in him could not stand to witness what he had done to that little girl. So he ran to his room plastered in pornography where he was safe.

Maria yelled for help, which came quickly. She was taken to the hospital in Nettuno and watched over by the parish priest there, a Spanish noble woman, two nuns and her mother. In the remaining hours of her life, this eleven-year-old girl could only think of where her mother would stay and how she would make out. She forgave Alessandro in no uncertain terms saying, "Yes, I forgive him and want him to be in Paradise with me some day." She was still concerned for his soul. She died on the 6th of July in 1902 at three o'clock in the afternoon, the hour of Mercy.

Grace and Mercy

Alessandro avoided being lynched on the spot through the intervention of the police. He was picked up for the murder, tried and sentenced to thirty years in prison. For eight years of his thirty-year sentence he was the same hard, petulant boy in a man's body. However, one night in that eighth year he had a dream.

Alessandro was one who never remembered his dreams. So when he "awoke" within this dream, he noted right away just how real it seemed, how aware he was even when the all-too-familiar cell melted away. He was suddenly in a field filled with flowers. A peasant girl approached him dressed in white. He thought it strange that she was dressed so. Then he noticed it was little Maria.

Alessandro tried to run again. That puerile urge to flee responsibility and interior pain leaped up again. He wanted to escape, but he couldn't. As in many people's dreams, his legs would not move. Maria approached him and handed him lilies, the flower of pure chastity. He took them. He took all fourteen of them, the same number as the times he had stabbed her.

Then Maria said to him with a kind of firm confidence, "Alessandro, as I have promised, your soul shall someday reach me in heaven." And with those words, the wounded boy from Ferriere lost the bitterness of soul that had plagued him since youth. He now hoped. Perhaps even he could be loved, loved and saved. He awoke a completely changed man.

Alessandro remained in prison for twenty-seven of the thirty-year sentence. He was released early due to good behavior. When he left, he wandered for a time but ended up with Capuchins in Macerata, Italy, going to daily Mass with the friars who called him "brother." After eight years, Alessandro mustered enough courage to travel to Corinaldo to see Assunta, Maria's mother.

On Christmas of 1937 he begged her forgiveness, which she gave with the same grace that her daughter showed. Then, with the kind of astonishing fortitude that should make everyone question their own mettle, the mother of the murdered girl walked with Alessandro, holding the murderer's hand in her own, pulling him to Mass like a mother does her son. The son follows because he must and because he wants to. Then there, at the altar rail, they knelt side-by-side to receive our dear Lord Jesus Christ, body, blood, soul and divinity. Assunta would say that she could never, would never have done this without the model of her departed daughter who demonstrated the same mercy.

On June 24th, 1950 Pope Pius XII would canonize Maria Goretti for her testament to the virtue of chastity and fortitude. It was the first time in history that the mother was present at a saint's canonization. It was also, as the Holy Father put it, the first time that St. Peter's was "hopelessly inadequate" to contain the mass of humanity that had come out to celebrate the life of Maria Goretti.

At one point, Pope Pius veered from his script and cried out, "What this little girl did, are you Christian people prepared to imitate?" To this the crowd responded loudly, "We are." And the Holy Father could do nothing but to pause and wipe the tears from his eyes at the sight and sound of grace and mercy on earth.

A Convicting Virtue

At her beatification Pope Pius XII said that Maria stood for much more than victimhood. She stood for the acceptance of poverty, for obedience, for sacrifices of love, for a dedication to the Eucharist and for forgiveness.

We may be tempted to think once again that St. Maria Goretti was a saint because she lost her life in a struggle for purity. This would be a mistake. Cardinal Salotti, the Prefect of the Congregation of Rites at the time of Maria's beatification stated that "even had she not been a martyr she would still have been a saint, so holy was her everyday life."[28] We must realize that the struggle she had against Alessandro would have ended much differently, or would never have taken place, had not Maria been in the habit of chastity and fortitude, a habit she fostered diligently well before her encounter with the broken boy that day.

Virtues are habits won through determination and grace. Sanctity is a life lived. It is not a closing blip on life's pursuits. St. Maria Goretti did what she did and is the model for us because she first loved Christ and did so with consistency. She is a saint because she learned through constant prayer and meditation about the value of a love that can say no to evil.

Santa Maria would rather have died than sin or agree to another's sin. She would rather have been killed at the hands of a neighbor than to allow him to offend the sweet Lord whom she loved so dearly. Her witness in life would be considered the height of lunacy today, but the world is a poor judge of what passes for sanity.

What are we willing to do? What sins cross our transom so often that we are no longer even sensitized to them? What are we doing to help turn the tide that continues to objectify our daughters, sisters, nieces and friends at younger and younger ages? When will we stop pretending that pornography, in its many forms, does not add to the culture of death that takes the lives of innocent girls like Maria? Would we answer Pope Pius XII in the same way as the many thousands did that day she was canonized?

Whatever we do or don't do, let us pray for the intercession of St. Maria Goretti. Let us pray that the girl of eleven years can teach us something about moral fortitude in the face of danger. Let us pray that we might be willing to risk at least a little embarrassment for the truth, so that we can some-day be with little Maria in Paradise.

St. Maria Goretti pray for us, and long live Christ the King.

Prayer

Dear Maria, when did you forgive? Was it right away? How could you have forgiven your murderer? How is it that Our Lord can ask us to turn the other cheek, to love our enemies and forgive those who hate us? Did he teach you that lesson himself? Was that what you learned as you contemplated his death on the cross?

Dear Maria, help us to pray. Give us your childlike trust in the power of prayer so that we might give over to Jesus all of our anxiety and all of our fear. Help us to forgive! Help us to open our heart to the Divine Physician, our Lord Jesus, so that we can forgive and be unburdened.

And dear Maria, help us to escape the chains of sin that have wrapped up our lives. Help us to be pure. Help us to have the fortitude you had. Help us say no to the world, to turn off the machines that draw us away from Jesus, from the Jesus who so yearns to embrace us. Oh dear Maria, pray that we might be saints so as to build a civilization of love here on earth and then, with Alessandro, meet you in heaven alongside our Lord Jesus Christ. Amen.

Compendium

570. ...*Faced with the many situations involving fundamental and indispensable moral duties, it must be remembered that Christian witness is to be considered a*

fundamental obligation that can even lead to the sacrificing of one's life, to martyrdom in the name of love and human dignity.[29]   The history of the past twenty centuries, as well as that of the last century, is filled with martyrs for Christian truth, witnesses to the faith, hope and love founded on the Gospel. Martyrdom is the witness of one who has been personally conformed to Jesus crucified, expressed in the supreme form of shedding one's blood according to the teaching of the Gospel: if "a grain of wheat falls into the earth and dies ... it bears much fruit" (Jn 12:24).

245. *The situation of a vast number of the world's children is far from being satisfactory, ...* Moreover, some serious problems remain unsolved: trafficking in children, child labor, the phenomenon of "street children", the use of children in armed conflicts, child marriage, the use of children for commerce in pornographic material, also in the use of the most modern and sophisticated instruments of social communication. It is essential to engage in a battle, at the national and international levels, against the violations of the dignity of boys and girls caused by sexual exploitation, by those caught up in pedophilia, and by every kind of violence directed against these most defenseless of human creatures.[30]   These are criminal acts that must be effectively fought with adequate preventive and penal measures by the determined action of the different authorities involved.

VII

SINNER AND SAINT, ST. THOMAS BECKET

There is something appealing about the playboy-turned-good-guy story so common in our time. Redemption is always a popular story line, but even more popular is the idea of instant redemption, the kind where someone suddenly overcomes years of vicious habits and chooses the good. It is a happy thing to think that we can live as we want to now. Then later, much later, we might turn our lives around in an instant and just in time to be met by a smiling Jesus.

This contemporary narrative is played out in hundreds of movies and television shows. Characters that are loathsome in the typically acceptable ways suddenly have a fit of conscience and "do the right thing." They might be brutal killers, hit men for the mob who draw the line at killing children. Then, as the typical story goes, our "hero" is ordered to kill a child who has "seen too much," and so the hit man is moved to suddenly seek a life of peace.

Pushed too far by his former employers, he decides to kill all the bad guys in stupefying displays of bloodletting. Somehow, in our culture of anemic moral reasoning, killing only the bad guys is considered virtue. Thus are our modern heroes made. But this is illusion. Virtue is hard fought and the fruit of regular habit.

Remembered every December 29th, as we recover from the Christmas reveries and prepare for the New Year, St. Thomas Becket's example ought to teach us something different about how lives are turned around. A scan of his life reveals that he was a man who struggled with himself. He often failed, but he longed to be good and so would begin anew each time. He sought the graces and took the necessary steps that could make sanctity possible, but he did not suddenly turn his life around. Sanctity, despite what our world will tell us, is not a store-bought accessory to life. It is the constant effort to improve our selves for the sake of Jesus, or rather it is the constant decision to allow Jesus to improve us.

The Good Life

Born in 1118 to parents of some means, Becket's life from the start was of some notable difference when compared to that of the other St.

Thomas of England, Thomas More. Whereas More's parents were careful never to encourage in their son any sort of profligate tendency, Thomas Becket became very used to "the good life" early. He had no real employment even into his twenties, a relatively advanced age.

This part of Thomas' story reminds one of some youth of today who, well-advanced in years, live at home for lack of initiative. They are comfortable not doing much of anything. With so many possible choices for employment, career or vocation there is no urgency in choosing any one path immediately. Wealth can have a stultifying effect on the will, a truth that bears itself out in the life of St. Thomas.

His wealthy parents died when he was twenty-one, and the young Thomas found that he needed to start to support himself. He was able to do so through a good position with a relative in London. This connection won him employers like Richer de l'Aigle, from whom he learned the very worldly pleasures of hawking and hunting. After that, at the age of twenty-four, he managed to attain a post in the household of the Archbishop of Canterbury, Theobold.

The Archbishop, as was typical of the time, was a master of a vast network of castles and important lands. Taking a liking to the young Thomas, His Grace Theobold made sure the lad had several niceties and creature comforts. He was granted minor orders. In 1154 he was ordained a deacon, then named the archdeacon of Canterbury, the most important ecclesial post in England after the bishops and abbots. This was a position that came with many benefits, among them a great social circle that included royalty.

This meteoric rise of Thomas was due to several things. Thomas knew when to keep quiet for one. His temperament was suited to the work. When he spoke, he was always frank but diplomatic. He had a sharp mind, with which he could make complicated issues simpler and more manageable for those he served. Though sometimes prone to impetuous acts in his personal life, usually associated with the pursuit of bodily pleasures, Thomas was measured in his advice. He always knew the right course of action, even if he did not always follow it himself.

These aspects of his character were forever helpful to Archbishop Theobold. More importantly for England's monarchy, it was Thomas who was sent to Rome by the Archbishop in order to secure the pope's blessing on royal succession. Henry of Anjou would succeed King Stephen instead of Eustace. In part thanks to Thomas' diplomatic skill, he guaranteed the throne for Henry II and restored the Plantagenet line of William the Conqueror. As a reward, he was made Chancellor of all of England in 1155.

The King's Man

The chancellorship of England brings up another difference between Becket and St. Thomas More. The latter was a friend of Henry VIII in the way that a subject could be a friend to such a meg-alomaniacal monarch. Thomas More respected his king and loved him as a loyal subject but never considered himself to be anything more than a plaything in the king's eyes. Becket's relationship with Henry II, however, was more like a bosom friend. In private they joked and played like schoolboys.

Misery, particularly the misery of sin, loves company. The younger Henry would encourage Thomas to vice and so Becket accepted every chance to embrace the trappings of his position. He engaged in all sorts of sins, venial and mortal. Once gambling, drinking, ostentation, excess, political subterfuge and siding with Henry against the Church were regular to Thomas' routine, it was naturally easier for him to engage in the deadly sins of lust and fornication.

Like many things of this world, a sinful slide into debauchery wins praise and friends. So Becket eventually landed the rank of general in the king's army. He fought for the crown in order to regain the land of Toulouse. He wore armor, led charges, designed attacks and even engaged in hand-to-hand combat, which men of the cloth were specifi-cally barred from doing.

His lifestyle as Lord High Chancellor was quite extravagant. On a trip to France for the sake of the king, Becket's retinue included some two-hundred persons. Who else, after all, would take care of the "eight wagon loads of presents, music and singers, hawks and hounds, monkeys and mastiffs," not to mention the two wagons dedicated to carrying beer to the French, who it was said preferred it to their own wine?

Such a traveling caravan is appropriate perhaps for a representative of the king who must project the king's power, influence and wealth. The French reacted to Thomas' entourage by saying, "If this is the chancellor's state, what can the king's be like?"[31]

Perhaps all this ostentation was appropriate for the chancellor. However, Thomas was an arch-deacon, a significant cleric within the Church in England. While he had no vow of poverty, this extravagance would count as scandal. Certainly, the gambling and the drinking and the rest are occasions of great sin and violations of Our Lord's trust. Thomas was allowing his station as the king's man to go to his head.

All of this marked St. Thomas' exterior life, but we still see glimpses of an interior conscience pricked with guilt. He is not altogether corrupt. He was a man who, like many of us, wishes to be better than he is. At times, Thomas would retreat to Merton, England near Exeter in order to pray and be silent. We hear that he would take "the discipline," i.e. he would engage in self-flagellation. He would seek out his confessor with regularity. He was an all-too-human man who struggled with his own will.

One can almost imagine the sorts of lies Thomas told himself about his life, lies that included the insistence that his extravagance was necessary while he represented the king. His prayers were perhaps much like St. Augustine's, that other great "playboy" of the West. "Give me virtue Lord, but not yet."

Nevertheless, it was most definitely Thomas Becket's conscience that drove him to these practices of penance. And it was this healthy conscience that also compelled him to decline to become the Archbishop of Canterbury when King Henry II asked it. Archbishop Theobold died in 1161, and Henry could think of no better person to take the Archbishop's chair than his bosom friend Thomas.

As Chancellor, Thomas had taken the king's side on a number of ecclesiastical matters. King Henry no doubt thought that with Thomas as the head of the Church in England, he would have complete control over the Church. He could then count on its influence and wealth to supply his own efforts, just as his forefathers had in the early days after the Norman Conquest.

Thomas knew, however, that should he become Archbishop, he would be duty-bound to defend the Church's interests over the crown's. What's more, with the new responsibility as

Archbishop, he could no longer live the life of leisure to which he had become accustomed. So, a desperate Thomas fought with Henry and even the pope about succeeding Theobold. Eventually, the pope demanded it, and Thomas accepted, resigning the chancellorship in the process. He became Archbishop the week after Pentecost Sunday 1162, which he then made the feast of the Holy Trinity, years before it was celebrated as such by the wider Church.

The Church's Man

Immediately, Thomas began the hard work of changing his life. He went to bed earlier in order to rise sooner and study Scripture. He surrounded himself with holy priests and friends, a practice from which we could all learn. He was moderate in food and drink. He learned to begin real service towards others by visiting the monks in the infirmary and spending time with the poor who came to his door.

What's more, he made sure that those seeking the priesthood were nothing like he was. A man petitioning Holy Orders would have to prove his character. Not even a request from the king could whitewash the terrible particulars in a candidate's background. If there was no holiness of life, there was no hope for ordination.

The first year of Archbishop Thomas' reign was relatively quiet. There were some matters of conflict with the king which caused some perturbances at the royal palace but nothing of great note. Then arose the famous case of the canon Philip de Brois. Philip was accused of murder and was acquitted by an ecclesial court but then brought before Simon Fitzpeter, the king's man. De Brois not only refused to be involved in a trial by the state, he dared to insult Fitzpeter. Thomas and Henry fought bitterly over this insult. Henry gave way but was never satisfied. His plan for Thomas was not working out as he had hoped.

The king then called a council at Westminster wherein he demanded that any clergy accused of a crime should be brought before the civil courts for punishment. Some of the English bishops wavered, but it was Thomas who held them fast to the rights of the Church. The king then demanded that the bishops accept his "royal customs." Thomas said he would, to a point, but this proved to be a disastrous mistake.

Perhaps it was his friendship with Henry. Perhaps it was a temporary lack of judgment. Perhaps it was just the general weakness of character with which he still struggled. The king had begun to take land away from Thomas, land he had been gifted many years prior. Perhaps this was the old Thomas who, in fear of losing his precious wealth, gave in ever-so-slightly to the king. Whatever the reason, Becket gave to the king the opportunity to define which of his "royal customs" the Church would have to recognize. He provided the king a foothold, but then, that is all a king needs to abuse the Church. Just the slightest bit of license is all an enemy of the Church requires to do ill against her.

When the "royal customs" were finally laid out, Thomas realized his error. Henry II demanded the right previously held by Henry I, son of William the Conqueror, to have the final say on whether clerics could leave England, on any appeal to Rome and on excommunications. Also, when a bishopric was vacant, the king would take charge and thus receive any and all benefits that would go to the bishop until a replacement was found, which was in part also up to the king. Finally, clerics accused of a crime were to be put before the civil courts for punishment, a situation which would invariably have led to double punishments. Archbishop Thomas Becket refused to agree to such terms, and the war between the two friends broke out in earnest.

The Hunted Priest

Thomas' error created a situation for the Church to have to say "no" to the king. He knew very well what Henry's aim was. It was foolish of him to have put himself and the other bishops of England in this tenuous position. What's more, he provided corrupt bishops the means with which to lobby for their own cause and ingratiate themselves with the king against the interests of the Church.

He is reported to have said at the time, "I am a proud, vain man, a feeder of birds and a follower of hounds, and I have been made a shepherd of sheep. I am fit only to be cast out of the see which I fill." [32]

For the next forty days and nights, he refused to say Mass, finding himself unworthy. He refused to wear his mitre or pallium. He fasted and prayed and made reparations as best he could. He sent word to the pope to seek forgiveness and to ask for the permission to step down as Archbishop. Meanwhile, King Henry only increased the pressure on Thomas. He took away more land, sued the Church and got other bishops to turn on Thomas.

At a council at Northhampton, called by the king, Thomas was to be judged by his old friend Henry. Becket appeared at the council and said to the assembly of English bishops:

"Judgment? I was given the church of Canterbury free from temporal obligations. I am therefore not liable and will not plead concerning them.

"You are bound to obey God and me before your Earthy king. Neither law nor reason allows children to judge their father and condemn him. Wherefore I refuse the king's judgment and yours and everybody's; under God, I will be judged by the pope alone. You, my fellow bishops, who have served man rather than God, I summon to the presence of the pope. And so, guarded by the authority of the Catholic Church and the Holy See, I go hence."[33]

Thomas left the room and fled to France with the sound of his brother bishops yelling "traitor" filling his ears. It was October of 1164.

In France, Becket was received by King Louis VII and was delivered to Pope Alexander III who happened to be passing through Sens. By the time Thomas could arrive, the English bishops aligned with Henry II had already told the pope their side of the story. The Holy Father was inclined to accept their testimony. But when Thomas showed the pope the text of the king's demands, the pope agreed the situation was dire. Though he sided with Thomas, he scolded him for his foolishness. He also refused to allow him to give up as Archbishop of Canterbury.

This is another interesting aspect of this life. Many of us have the tendency, when we have failed, to give up, to turn back, to lose hope. Such an attitude is usually the result of pride and not humility. It is the proud man who thinks that they never make mistakes. It is the humble man who, when confronted with their own inevitable failure, turns rather to God and continues with good work. Thomas was still learning the life of sanctity, still struggling to be a good man and it was the Holy

Father who helped Becket remain true to his duty. Sanctity is slow work.

Thomas Becket hid in France for the next six years, constantly pursued by the king. His friends and family in England were persecuted or sent into exile where he was hiding. Thomas knew he had to return to relieve their suffering, but he also knew he had to act boldly.

Becket decided to excommunicate the bishops of York, London and Salisbury for having conspired to coronate the son of Henry II against the rights of Canterbury. This got the king's attention.

Thomas met with Henry his old friend in Normandy, France in 1170. The meeting was cordial enough. There was hope that things would be different. Henry gave way a bit and invited Thomas back, perhaps in the hopes that the excommunications would be lifted. So Thomas came back to his cathedral in November of that year.

The people of England received Thomas well. When he visited London, they came out into the streets to cheer the Archbishop who stood up to the king. So it was that instead of lifting the excommunications, Thomas maintained them.

News of this reached Henry II, who was still in France on a campaign, and it was at this time that the fateful words were uttered in a fit of rage by Henry Plantagenet, King of England, "What sluggards, what cowards have I brought up in my court, who care nothing for the allegiance to their lord. Will no one rid me of this meddlesome priest?"

Becket Serves His King

These words were interpreted by Reginald Fitzurse, William de Tracy, Richard le Breton and Hugh de Morville as a call to kill Thomas. Their plot was no secret, and Thomas had received threats to his life before. This latest situation was different. Thomas was sure of the outcome here and knew that he deserved no better end after his failures to guard and protect the Church against a king so vicious.

On December 29th, 1170 the Archbishop of Canterbury, Thomas Becket, was in the cathedral accompanied only by Edward Grim, a visiting monk from Cambridge who had been a long-time friend of Thomas'. The beautiful house of God was populated by a small crowd as well as by the monks attached to the cathedral praying and preparing for Vespers, the evening prayer. When Thomas entered, they were happy to see him alive and rose to bar the doors of the church, but Thomas stopped them saying, "It is not proper that a house of prayer, a church of Christ, be made a fortress, since although it is not shut up, it serves as a fortification for his people; we will triumph over the enemy through suffering rather than by fighting - and we come to suffer, not to resist."

The four knights entered the cathedral of

Canterbury accompanied by a fifth man, Hugh the Evil-cleric, named so by history because of his particularly heinous part in the crime. They demanded to see the Archbishop, the traitor. Thomas approached them, identifying himself as a priest not a traitor. They then attacked him most violently.

The first blow was to the head and its follow-through injured Grim, who held up Thomas while others fled. It was the third blow that caused Thomas to buckle and fall. He cried out, "For the name of Jesus and in defense of the Church I am willing to die." Thomas was prostrate now, face down before the high altar just as those who are about to be ordained to Holy Orders lay down as they prepare to give their lives up to the Church.

The fourth blow was the decisive one, made worse by the evil cleric Hugh who dug his heel into Thomas' remains. All four knights had a hand in the evil deed. Only Hugh de Morville did not strike a single blow against the Archbishop. Rather, he scattered the onlookers to prevent anyone else coming to Thomas' aid.

The sacrilege of the event shocked the people into a temporary silence and inaction. This shock prevented them from even approaching the body. What was left of Thomas lay on the floor of the Cathedral for some days. But the people of England knew the significance of this immediately. They knew for what Thomas was murdered. They understood that this was about the defense of the

Church over the aggression of the State. Some considered it the just end of a profligate man and Archbishop. However, the people discovered a good deal about Thomas after his death.

Sinner and Saint

They discovered that St. Thomas wore a hair shirt underneath his ecclesial robes. He had doubled the amount given to the poor when he became Archbishop. He had spent many hours in private prayer and sacrifice. Thomas' confessor reported that, though tempted often with all sorts of opportunities for corruption and scandal, the late Archbishop never succumbed. After learning of all of this about Thomas the vicious man, the playboy, the all-too-human servant of God, the people of England understood that all along he had been a man in pursuit of sanctity and that he had found it in death. Indeed, they discovered that he had returned to England despite a vision from our Lord that he would be martyred there.

For all his failures, St. Thomas Becket was after all a man who sought true love at the bosom of Christ. He struggled through life, climbing the ladder. He never really had any dear friends, friends who could help him find wholeness. He was just like those of us who seek our own wills against the interests of the Kingdom of God. It was not until he turned himself over to Christ that he discovered his own mettle and the way to seek the

Kingdom here on Earth.

By the people of England and by the Church, Thomas was made a saint immediately. Henry II was forced to give public penance. And we are gifted by our Church with several lessons.

We learn that sanctity does not simply come about without some prior efforts and graces. Though we might like to believe in the sudden turn-around, a change that happens instantaneously, life is very seldom like that. Little steps must be made all along the way. Even St. Paul, who was struck blind in order to turn his life around, still had to receive instruction from the Apostles before he began his ministry.

St. Thomas was not a sudden convert. He did not have the implausible change in character that Hollywood assures us happens. His was a constant effort to be better than he was. He felt pain with every failure to live up to the Christ he believed in, so he frequented the sacrament of confession, which is a good lesson for all those who seek the life of holiness. When he left for retreat in Merton, he was removing himself from the temptations and trappings of everyday life. So he teaches us that a regular retreat is also a good rule of life.

We learn through St. Thomas about hope. We learn that we are never totally lost while we live. We must always pursue the holy life, and when we fail we must re-double that pursuit. Christ, our true King, would have it no other way. Faced with the daunting tasks of poverty and the myriad of social ills in this world, we can still hope that our little efforts, our small part will make a difference.

One of the more important lessons we learn from St. Thomas Becket is the importance of little efforts against our tendency towards avarice. So much of our society is caught up with having more stuff. The allure of things entrap us and pull us away from the kind of person we hope to be. This was the case for Thomas who struggled to say goodbye to his life of leisure.

We are often unaware of how much of a hold our things have on us. It is a kind of slavery, and worse it numbs the conscience. It is more difficult, the Church continues to teach us, to hear the cries of the poor when we are so caught up maintaining our stuff. We sometimes assume that the rich man in Christ's parable was intentionally callous to Lazarus the beggar who sat outside his front gate. But there is nothing in the story that would necessarily suggest that. The rich man could have simply been too distracted with his sumptuous meals to notice the beggar. That is, Christ teaches us, the danger of things.

So St. Thomas also teaches us that sometimes the best remedy for dealing with material attachments is to make a clean break, for things have a tendency to speak to us when we are thinking about parting with them. They somehow worm their way into our minds to tell us that they will be useful someday, or that we deserve them. True, beautiful things are not bad because they are beautiful or expensive. But so long as they occupy a space in our psyches they stand as an obstacle between us and heaven, they must be plucked out of our lives. We must steel ourselves in order to simplify our lives. It is hard work, but it must be done.

Finally, we learn that the rights of the Church must be defended to the utmost, for the State needs little excuse to abuse the Church. This is a lesson easily forgotten in our own day, when the comfort of things can convince us that all is well. The Church will always be powerful on some level because the Church brings Christ to the people. But it is because of this "power" that the State will always have a reason to grapple with the Church for influence, to limit what the Church can say and do.

Religious liberty, the freedom to pursue the dictates of our conscience within due limits, is a right for the Church and for individuals. Our increasingly secular culture sees the Church as an imposition on humanity, an obstacle to the progress of peoples. Where in some situations politicians claim that their conscience reigns supreme, when it comes to the conscience of the bishop or the Catholic business person, our government is increasingly callous.

Today, the Church's bishops find themselves, just as Thomas did, living in a steady tension between what the State claims is the common good and what the rights of the Church demand. The "royal customs" of our own day are creeping in upon the Church and faithful Catholics.

As always, the bishops are called to influence for a "common good" defined by a vision of the ultimate good. They are called to defend the right of religious liberty. We must pray, then, that our bishops stand as firm as St. Thomas Becket did to the end.

Let us also pray that we have the courage to lay down our own lives for the Church, for we have no king but the one of Heaven. Woe to that Catholic who turns his or her back on the Church's rights in the name of whatever earthly lord of whatever party. As Dorothy Day once said, we must never replace Holy Mother Church for "Holy Mother the State."[34] Long live Christ the King.

Prayer

Dear Thomas, teach us how to reject our own sins so that we might focus on the Lord. Our distractions are always before us. Please pray that we have the wisdom and prudence to better walk the path to sanctity. Help us to love well. Help us, too, to muster the strength to speak the truth when it is necessary. Help us to get over our fear of social martyrdom. Help us be witnesses worthy of the name Christian. Help us preach the Gospel always, in action and in word.

St. Thomas Becket, help us to come to Jesus in the confessional and to pour out to him our failures. Help us to learn from your hard-won lessons and not to flee from the God who desires only our good. And help us be like your friend Edward Grim who, instead of running away, stayed with you to help support his Church. Help us to defend our Church against the false kings of today. Amen.

Compendium

328. *Goods, even when legitimately owned, always have a universal destination; any type of improper accumulation is immoral, because it openly contradicts the universal destination assigned to all goods by the Creator.* Christian salvation is an integral liberation of man, which means being freed not only from need but also in respect to possessions. "For the

love of money is the root of all evils; it is through this craving that some have wandered away from the faith" (*1 Tim 6:10*). The Fathers of the Church insist more on the need for the conversion and transformation of the consciences of believers than on the need to change the social and political structures of their day. They call on those who work in the economic sphere and who possess goods to consider themselves administrators of the goods that God has entrusted to them.

360. *The phenomenon of consumerism maintains a persistent orientation towards "having" rather than "being".* This confuses the "criteria for correctly distinguishing new and higher forms of satisfying human needs from artificial new needs which hinder the formation of a mature personality"[35]. To counteract this phenomenon it is necessary to create "life-styles in which the quest for truth, beauty, goodness and communion with others for the sake of common growth are the factors which determine consumer choices, savings and investments"[36]. It is undeniable that ways of life are significantly influenced by different social contexts, for this reason the cultural challenge that consumerism poses today must be met with greater resolve, above all in consideration of future generations, who risk having to live in a natural environment that has been pillaged by an excessive and disordered consumerism.[37]

POSTSCRIPT: One of the chilling notes about this story is what happened to those four knights involved with this heinous murder: Reginald Fitzurse, William de Tracy, Richard le Breton and Hugh de Morville. It is reported that all four were excommunicated and sent to the Holy Land to make a penitential amends for their crime. All four are said to have died alone, that is without loved ones or a priest, and the three who struck the Archbishop suffered violent deaths betrayed by their own companions.

VIII

COMMUNION AND
ST. ISIDORE OF SEVILLE

In the list of forgotten saints, which grows ever longer with every passing age, is one of the most amazing saints for our time. His feast is on April 4th. His name is St. Isidore of Seville. He composed one of the oldest liturgies still in use today and popularized the study of Aristotle in Europe, well before St. Albert or St. Thomas ever did. His mind was so encyclopedic that he is where we got the idea of an encyclopedia, since he was the first to write one. It is this fact that makes him the patron of computers, computer users and the internet. But more than any of that, St. Isidore was a man who understood the importance of culture and of communion, words which are at the heart of Catholic social teaching.

A Steady Effort

Isidore was born around the year 560 in Cartagena, a major naval port in southeastern Spain. Two of his brothers, Leander and Fulgentius, became saints, and their sister, Florentina, became a saint by founding many convents.

Their father Severianus, probably a Roman nobleman, was married to Theodora, who was descended of the Visigoths. It was a mixed marriage of sorts. The Visigoths had conquered Spain a century before, and they were still not entirely on friendly terms with the native Roman culture. At any rate, Severianus' background meant that the young Isidore was placed in the cathedral school of Seville. This was a rare opportunity since the Visigoths rejected the educational traditions of the Romans.

At the school, Isidore found himself under the tutelage of his older brother Leander, who was a stern master. Failures of memorization were opportunities for Leander to punish him. We can imagine that perhaps the young Isidore hoped from time to time that the Visigoths had done a better job of eliminating the classical arts. He did not care for the dull repetitiveness of Latin and Greek. Indeed, those studies have rarely ever been met with joy by any child. So, like many throughout history who have had to apply their wit and will power to those ancient languages, Isidore waivered. Actually, he ran away.

He ran to the seaside, and while at the edge of the Mediterranean Sea, Isidore noticed something spectacular. Along with the waters glistening with the reflection of the sun, and along with the loveliness of birds gliding on the invisible, he noticed gigantic stones with holes worn straight through them. Water, which has no firmness to it, wore away the hardness of stone over time with patient, undeterred and constant dripping, moment after moment, year upon year. What is more, he noticed that the holes were not jagged with dangerous edges, the result of some crash or trauma. These holes were smoothly wrought over time. They had a softness to them. They were made to look beautifully crafted.

Isidore grasped instantly an important truth of life, one which escapes some of the brighter human lights of today. He realized that, like those large stones on the seaside, his stony heart and nature could be formed through determined constancy into something beautiful for God. He realized the potential within himself if, by means of regular effort, he could allow his spirit to be fashioned into something glorious. The realization gave the young lad the impetus to return to the repetitive lessons which his older brother gave him, for he now knew that he was studying not just language but the stuff of virtue, the opportunity for human development.

This truth Isidore encountered is key to the social teaching of the Church. It is an important truth for what it says about the nature of the human person, and the social teaching is nothing if it is not founded on the Church's understanding of the human experience. The principles in the social teaching are important, but they are only half the story. The human condition is such that, as we try to live up to those principles, we regularly struggle against our baser instincts.

So it is not enough to simply know the doctrine, the encyclicals and the principles. For the social teaching to work we need men and women of virtue, people who can actually act on the truth that they know in their own heads, and this requires regular effort. The virtues, which are simply good habits, help us to know the good, understand how best to achieve the good and avoid extremes in either direction that keep us from doing the good. With them well in hand, achieving something approaching the common good is finally possible. But we cannot develop our virtues without practice.

St. Paul famously asked why it was that he failed to do that which he wanted and ended up doing that which he hated (Rm. 7:15). We all experience this because it is part of the human condition to fight against ourselves. The thinkers of the Enlightenment called it alienation. The spiritualists of the East call it a misalignment. Christians call it sin, and it is at the heart of every social ill. Sin is the root cause of social injustice. To combat it we need the grace of Christ.

However, as St. Augustine would have argued, grace needs to work on nature and our natures are weak. For this reason, virtue needs to be pursued. We need the kind of constant, regular decision for the good that is the foundation of a good life. Isidore realized that anything was possible with enough patient persistence for the good.

Living the social teaching of the Church is the same thing. It is a constant decision for the good, for the whole good and the good of every person in every aspect of our lives. It is not sufficient to be virtuous in our sexual lives and ignore the immoralities of consumption. Neither is it sufficient to be virtuous in our environmental choices if we simultaneously ignore the immoralities of abortion and contraception. The Catholic life of virtue is a whole, a united thing that touches all of our life every day. We must strive for virtue in all things.

The Fractured Society

Through his regular study, Isidore would become one of the most learned men in all of Spain, but he was devout as well. We need a nature crafted by virtue, but more than that we need the graces Christ offers us. Though he never became a monk himself, Isidore became an educator in their schools and helped draw up a rule of life for the monks which was adopted throughout Spain. He understood that the monastic dedication to formation and to virtue at the service of Christ is the foundation for a holy society. The key to the happy life about which the philosophers wrote may be virtue, but the key to a holy life is Christ Jesus. Isidore saw that the monks lived authentic lives by striking the proper order and balance between philosophy and the spiritual life. The monastic movement would be a key player in his work for Spain.

Still, not all was perfect in the monasteries. Isidore was greatly concerned with the distinctions within monasteries between freemen and slaves. Sometimes even our monasteries suffer from the influences of the world. He insisted, then, that no such distinctions be made.

This is a departure from the philosophy of Aristotle and even Plato who would argue that certain men are made to be slaves, they are incapable of the higher life as is obvious because of their state in life. Isidore understood the folly of this. He, a Catholic prelate of the 6th and 7th century, totally rejected the notion that slavery was justifiable. The Kingdom of God does not permit such divisions. It is a Kingdom of communion, and so that should be the model for the city of man.

Eventually, Isidore would assist his brother Leander, who was later the Archbishop of Seville, and around the year 600 would succeed him as the head of the Church in southern Spain. In his role as archbishop, Isidore was concerned with communion. So it was that St. Isidore became a champion of education, for he was a stalwart defender of the power and liberty which education provides, its influence on culture and unity and its absolute necessity for any healthy society.

Spain in the 7th century was a mass of competing races and languages. It was a divided kingdom which lacked a sense of communion that would have made sense of the common good. There were, first of all, the Spanish Romans who had been part of the Empire for centuries. But Roman rule of the land would end in the 5th century. The Vandals sacked Rome in 455 and ran their path into Spain. They were not too long afterwards conquered by the Visigoths, who made their mark rather quickly and influenced much of Isidore's life. Different languages and legal structures for the different peoples meant that the world he grew up in was a fractured one

The Goths and Vandals were united in one important way, however: many were Arians. Arians insisted that Jesus was not God. The Council of Nicaea settled the matter, and the orthodox Church expunged Arians from the Empire. But when the exiled were driven out of the Church, many went North and converted the Germanic Vandals and Goths. Thus it was that these very same Arian Visigoths ruled Spain when little Isidore was born, and thus it was that the divisions ran deeply through his society. They were cultural and political divisions but also spiritual.

The Visigoths eventually gave up on Arianism, and the separate legal systems which had been set up for Romans and Goths did end during Isidore's life. However, the culture was still fractured. It was, one could say, like the United States: an erstwhile melting pot that was regularly pulled apart from within by past wrongs and deep wounds. Isidore decided that as Archbishop of Seville he needed to gather his flock around him, and he laid out a plan. He would unite his people by means of education.

Unity through Education

A major aspect of Catholic social teaching seldom emphasized is the importance of education, not just as a means of drawing persons out of poverty but as a means of shaping culture. When the Church talks about implementing Catholic social teaching, she starts first with marriage and family and then moves not to public policy or economic structures but rather from family to culture. This importance of culture is a lesson Blessed Pope John Paul II taught many times. It is a foundation for communion and solidarity. What the Church teaches us is that neither is possible without a culture that provides art, cuisine, language, moral sensibilities, fashion, dance, religion, humor and so forth. Culture provides the building blocks for communion outside of our families.

Isidore understood that Spain required a cohesive culture. He knew that education was the means to achieve it, for education can provide the kind of common experience, language and ideals that can shape a culture's attitude towards the good, the true and the beautiful over the merely functional. Without a common sense of the good, there can be no united work towards the "common good" and thus no just society.

St. Isidore presided over the Fourth Council of Toledo, which required that all dioceses in Spain have a seminary. These seminaries would not content themselves with just the trivium and quadrivium, the ancient liberal arts, but they would also study medicine, law, Hebrew and Greek. Aristotle was required reading.

We often hear that Aristotle was introduced into the West by Islam in the 12th century. In fact, Aristotle was well known to educated Westerners thanks to St. Isidore and others, though it is true that copies of some important texts were not available until the time of St. Albert and St. Thomas Aquinas.

Isidore also understood that education requires information, information readily available to those interested in the truth. Therefore, to democratize access to information, St. Isidore wrote what amounts to one of the first encyclopedias. His "Etymologies" was so widely used and so well respected for its clarity and for covering such a wide breadth of information, that it was still read in the 16th century, a thousand years later. Here is a litany of some of the other of Isidore's achievements:

> "St. Isidore was a voluminous writer, his earlier works including a dictionary of synonyms, a treatise on astronomy and physical geography, a summary of the principal events of the world from the creation, a biography of illustrious men, a book of Old and New Testament worthies, his rules of monks, extensive theological and ecclesiastical works, and the history of the Goths, Vandals and Suevi."[38]

In fact it was St. Isidore's histories that are considered some of the most valued amongst his work, as they are some of the only histories we have of that time period and about those peoples.

St. Isidore stretches our understanding of service for the poor as well. The Archbishop of Seville loved the poor so much he not just feed them – his home was often surrounded by the poor and ill who sought aid from the holy bishop – but he also educated them about the beautiful things of this world, the very things that make us free. To feed a man is to meet his temporary need, but to educate him is to elevate his potential as a man.

About freedom we learn from our contemporary culture that it is the ability to do what we want, when we want, how we want. Isidore knew this was folly. Authentic freedom is the ability to do what is good. If we want to be free, to be the best versions of ourselves, we must be free to pursue our better angels. This will mean detachment from our slavery to things, and it means the ability to ignore the distractions of this world. But how will one know the good or how to distinguish between distractions and what matters unless through education?

This is why the liberal arts are called liberal, or liberating from the Latin *libertas*. By studying the lives and works of the brightest people in history, we can learn what is authentically good, what truly matters. If nothing else we can learn from their mistakes. In this way we are truly liberated, for by knowing the good, we can choose it and, by consistent choices for the good, become the best versions of ourselves, no longer shackled to our baser instincts or misconceptions about life.

His great love for learning and his ability to make so much knowledge available to so many are what earned him the patronage of computers, computer users and the internet. Would that we could exclusively use the internet to discover was is good and true. We ought certainly to pray to St. Isidore in order to protect the minds and souls of those who use the internet in our home.

St. Isidore's skills also included administration and organization. His system of councils in Spain, which he helped run for a time with his brother Leander, was hugely successful. The work he was able to perform to affect societal change was made possible through the conversations and diplomatic work he spearheaded. His willingness to include the Visigoths around the table, and his success at turning Spain away from delving into barbarism, was one of the greatest influences on Western representative government.

St. Isidore was proclaimed a Doctor of the Church in 1722 by Pope Benedict XIV and was often called the "Schoolmaster of the Middle Ages." He might also be called the proto Renaissance Man for his almost universal knowledge and expertise in so many disparate things. Whatever we call him, he would be most happy to be called a follower of Christ Jesus, a lover of Our Lady, a servant of the Church and a humble citizen in the Kingdom of Heaven.

Communion

This is certainly the core of St. Isidore. He was a man devoted to Christ Jesus and to his kingdom. Although he would help to structure a kingdom of men with the wisdom he offered kings and emperors, he was a man who also sought to build up God's kingdom above all things. He exemplifies in this way yet another aspect of the social teaching, namely the preference for communion over opposition.

It is another regular human habit to find reasons to disagree with each other when cooperation could do so much more good. Whether it is left vs. right, or rich vs. poor, or labor vs. management, we are trained practically from birth to think in terms of us vs. them. St. Isidore did all he could to encourage people to work towards communion. It seems every one of his efforts was to bring people together.

His creation of a liturgy which still exists today is a sign of that. The liturgy is an architecture of the heavenly kingdom, an imagining of the life to come, the life to which we are all invited, the life of ultimate communion. It is where we receive a foretaste of citizenship in our homeland. St. Isidore's liturgy is his lasting legacy. Known as the Mozarabic Rite, it is used even now in Toledo, Spain. Clips of it can be found, most appropriately, on the internet. But its impact at the time was its effect on communion. The liturgy is about Christ Jesus, about receiving him who draws all men to himself. Isidore understood this.

To be Catholic can mean "universal," but that does not fully capture it. For instance, opinion is universal in the sense that everyone has one, but there are as many opinions as there are people. Catholic is better understood as universal in the sense of being one. To be Catholic is to be unified, to be in communion, to share in the same thing, and it is this sharing that makes us universal.

The great mystery is that this unity is particular to us, respects our individuality while at the same time connecting us to each other. To be Catholic is to be in communion, to be, in the words of St. Augustine, "in some sort brothers."[39]

This is why the great divide in the Church between the "pro-life" Catholics and the "social justice" Catholics harms the Church to no end and undermines what it means to be Catholic. The fault is on both sides. Paradigms of conversation or action that pit one side against another, or encourage a laity vs. the hierarchy attitude must be rejected. That isn't communion. That isn't unity. That isn't Catholic.

St. Isidore of Seville teaches us that a life lived for communion requires a virtuous life drawn out through education. But he also points us back to the ultimate purpose of education, which is an invitation to an encounter with the Almighty.

Modern educational philosophies that ignore the spiritual and moral aspect of the human person are doomed to create technocratic citizens, who know only how to manipulate rules so as to create and master them for their own benefit. True education fosters what the ancients called *docilitas*, a docility or openness to learning. That openness is a key to the spiritual life and so must be fostered as much as possible, particularly in our land of comfort.

St. Isidore, who so wisely knew to place the Lord before any earthly princes, has a great deal to teach us. Let us pray that we learn to seek the truth above all things and strive to live with Christ, the King of our heavenly homeland.

Prayer

Dear Isidore, who suffered from the divisions in your world and strove for unity, how often in our own time are we pitted against each other? How often do we contribute to those divisions?

St. Isidore pray that we seek Christ Jesus in the Eucharist, the sacrament of communion. His love can heal all wounds. His call for unity can help us put aside our wants and desires, our commands for attention and recognition. Help us to love communion over our own wants, to love the Kingdom of God over our own victories and so be with you and Christ our joy forever in heaven.

Pray, too, that we might discover the true meaning of education, that we might be more willing to put aside the distractions of life in order rather to use our leisure time for what is true, good and beautiful. Help us always to work for your greater glory. Amen.

Compendium

242. *The family has the responsibility to provide an integral education.* Indeed, all true education "is directed towards the formation of the human person in view of his final end and the good of that society to which he belongs and in the duties of which he will, as an adult, have a share".[40] This integrality is ensured when children — with the witness of life and in words — are educated in

dialogue, encounter, sociality, legality, solidarity and peace, through the cultivation of the fundamental virtues of justice and charity.[41]

In the education of children, the role of the father and that of the mother are equally necessary.[42] The parents must therefore work together. They must exercise authority with respect and gentleness but also, when necessary, with firmness and vigor: it must be credible, consistent, and wise and always exercised with a view to children's integral good.

558. *The second challenge for Christian commitment concerns the content of culture, that is, truth.* The question of truth is essential for culture because "it remains each man's duty to retain an understanding of the whole human person in which the values of intellect, will, conscience and fraternity are pre-eminent".[43]

IX

SALVATION AND LABOR,
ST. JOSEPH THE WORKER

In the heady days of Communism, May 1st was made the major festival on which the common working man was finally given his due. When Lenin and his ilk were sure that it was only a matter of time before Communist zeal would usher in a global utopia, the worker was commemorated with pomp and circumstance. With the expansion of Communism, the festival spread the worldwide to become International Workers Day, and became opportunities to display the glories of the Communist effort. Celebrations included long lines of soldiers and weaponry, proof of the might of their movement.

It is not so much the same thing today, which is good and bad. That those displays of weapons of mass destruction are less common is a good thing. But today, International Worker's Day is a day for anarchists to display their deadly foolishness. May 1st is now associated not with the dignity of the proletariat or the nobility of the blue-collared family provider. It is more and more associated with hooliganism. Such is the resulting and inevitable descent brought about by atheist humanism.

We should be glad to know that the Church, which had been defending the rights of workers well before Lenin took over the Russian state in bloody style, did not idly stand by as the Communists claimed to protect the working man and woman. In 1955, Pope Pius XII erected the Feast of St. Joseph the Worker, which is celebrated on May 1st. The good pontiff hoped to draw attention to the Church's teaching on labor, a teaching that has continued to develop since Pope Leo XIII first wrote *Rerum novarum* on capital and labor in 1891.

With the feast, Pope Pius XII invites us to find the true meaning of work through St. Joseph. Meditation on Joseph and his example of Christian life reminds us that it was through labor that he worked out his salvation, and so teaches us a good deal about the social teaching of the Church.

Labor is Good

It seems difficult to make a case for the nobility of labor in our world. Communists really only pay lip service to it, for in the end they steal the fruits of labor. There is no private property, and so the laborer is alienated from his own work. This theft of the fruit of our labor is quintessentially dehumanizing, for we put part of ourselves in our work. The Communists do no favors for the working man when all is said and done. The gulags that spotted the Siberian tundra were the inevitable consequence of a state that thinks so little of man and his work.

This is not to say that the Western World's capitalism fairs that much better. It is increasingly corrupt and self-absorbed with its own wealth. Laborers are treated as means to an end, as things, as a commodity to be added up and quantified for the sake of maximizing profit. Profit is not evil, but treating workers as units of business is. Capitalism may not be fundamentally flawed, as is Communism, but left unchecked it tends towards serving the darker habits of the human spirit. Thus the free market tends to dehumanize as well. The slums about which Dickens wrote are the inevitable consequence of businesses that think so little of man and his work.

Defending the nobility of labor is also difficult because we tend to think of work as a curse on mankind. Many think that labor is a punishment given to us by an angry God because of the sin of Adam and Eve. The Garden of Eden was a place devoid of labor. The Earth simply provided man everything he needed, in a kind of magical utopia. This is why some argue that the first parents were vegetarians. It takes labor to cook up meat after all.

But all that is just nonsense.

Rehabilitating the dignity of labor, then, could start with looking again at Genesis. For despite what we might imagine about Adam and Eve, the truth is that when the good God created man, he put man to work right away. "The Lord God took the man and put him in the garden of Eden to till it and keep it." (Gen. 2:15) After this, the Lord formed the various animals to keep man company and then gave man the work of naming the animals.

Work is not foreign to man's nature. Whether it is the physical work of the field or the intellectual work of affixing names to reality, labor is part of what we were called to do from the beginning. Through it, we help to continue God's creative work in the world. How else would we have rendered adequate stewardship over the earth? How else would we have subdued the earth, but through labor?

This is one of Blessed John Paul II's points in his wonderful 1981 document on labor, *Laborem exercens*. There he explains that work is a good thing because through it we can participate in the creative power of God. Through work we help fulfill God's plan for creation. It was part of God's original plan to help us continue his work in the world. Instead of seeing your work as just some mundane task or just a means to pay the bills, realize that you are helping God create the world and move humanity through history. Starting a small business, beginning a project, forming a team, planning for the future of your work, managing a staff, all of that is creative work that, if done correctly, advances God's plan for salvation.

John Paul II also teaches us that through work we become more ourselves. Labor is a means by which we can tap into who we really are. God provides us with a nature that is inclined to labor and then calls us to a more specific work through a vocation. Our vocation, whether to the religious life or the lay or married states, is part of God's plan for our lives. In this way, then, a labor well done can deepen our commitment to faithful discipleship and advance our efforts toward salvation.

Good work requires virtue. Virtue is a good habit that can shape the soul. The virtue we seek is the virtue of industriousness, or the habit of conscientious labor. Conscientious labor is a work performed with one's responsibility towards God, towards his or her family, towards an employer and towards society in mind. It is work that is always a service. It is not frenetic behavior for the sake of getting something done. It is not merely enduring the present moment in order to receive a paycheck. Nor is it ever a wholly private activity. Rather, conscientious labor is work performed in deference to serving God and the world.

Conscientious labor, performed within the vocation to which God has called us, is always a blessing. One need not have to be a physician, teacher, lawyer or politician to consider their work significant enough to receive God's blessing. Any labor, by virtue of being a work freely chosen in obedience to God, can be an ennobling work and also salvific work.

St. Joseph the Worker

When we turn to St. Joseph we see the ultimate example of the laborer who responded to his vocation and to his responsibility to family and society. Acknowledging his duty to the State and society, St. Joseph moved his very pregnant spouse to Bethlehem in order to be counted as a member of his tribe. One could call this tribal loyalty rather than civic responsibility. Nevertheless, St. Joseph responded to the demands placed before him in the present moment with a "yes." St. Joseph's trust in God's Providence allowed the ancient prophesies to be fulfilled.

No doubt he labored in Bethlehem for a time until it became impossible for them to stay any longer, until the time came when they had to flee because of the vice of a king. Thus, while Our Lady provided Christ our Savior with the very flesh by which we were saved, St. Joseph made sure that flesh had enough to eat.

When it was time for Joseph and his family to flee Bethlehem for Egypt, he listened to the angel of the Lord, placed his trust in the Providence of God again and fled. He labored there in Egypt, a man in a foreign land seeking work to help his suffering family. We could no doubt learn a thing or two about the dignity of laborers in our nation who flee here for the hope of sustaining the life of families.

Once having returned from Egypt to Nazareth, St. Joseph would have taught the young Jesus what it was to work by the sweat of the brow. In this way, St. Joseph contributed to the humanity of Jesus and so contributed to our salvation. Through St. Joseph, Jesus came to understand industriousness, the very conscientious labor that seeks to feed a family, fulfill a contract and serve society. Thanks to St. Joseph's example of work, our own work today was redeemed in Jesus.

Consider what Blessed Mother Teresa had to say about St. Joseph:

"He was a just man; that means a holy man. He gave to God what belonged to him and to the creatures what belonged to them. Being 'just' means to give every person their due. We must show them love because they all belong to God. God loves us and the others also. We believe that we are tabernacles of the living God; the other sisters [of Charity] also; the people also. ...Saint Joseph [had] two talents – faithfulness and love – to serve Jesus. He was a common carpenter and became the foster Father of Jesus and spouse of the Mother of God. In all sincerity everybody must say I have used what I have got. I must be 'just' to others. ...People who want to become holy must pray to St. Joseph."[44]

St. Joseph was just because he was faithful to his God, to his family and to his vocation. This fidelity was made possible through love, and that love placed all that St. Joseph was and had and could do at the service of Jesus and Mary. He used what he received to be just, as Mother Teresa put it, and we now recognize him worldwide as a model for the just man.

St. Joseph knew that for this child and this woman he was given a task, a job, a vocation and he was to live and work and toil without counting the cost and without heeding the wounds. He gave what was due to Mary and Jesus, which was his work in carpentry, the work that provided for the home and fed and clothed them. He gave what was due to Christ Jesus, which of course was everything, his work and his masculinity, his example as a man and as a father, husband and provider. He gave what was due to their neighbors, who probably bought his wares in order to supply the needs for their own families. In training Jesus in the craft of carpentry, he served his neighbors who would benefit from the fruit of Jesus' labor, before he entered public ministry. St. Joseph was the just man, because he knew how much and to whom to give of himself. There is much to learn from this.

Justice and the Family

All parents struggle to live up to their own standards. We desire that, with the kind of sage and perfectly placed word, our children would hang on every piece of advice. We would like to be the prudent shopper who can squeeze a bit more out of a half-dollar. We would like to be the calm and self-composed adult in the room who never loses their cool. But we are not. Like St. Joseph, we are burdened by the same happy yokes of everyday life.

St. Joseph the Worker teaches us that when we stop trying to be the perfect parent and instead learn simply to say yes to what God is calling us to do right now, we become the parent we are supposed to be. If it means reading that children's book to our kids yet another time, if it means sitting down to study, if it means washing the dishes when we are ever-so-tired, if it means just listening, then it is all worthwhile labor. It is what the Lord wants right now, and it is therefore just and right and good. It is part of his plan. It is part of our salvation.

The principle carries forward to the work in the factory, the work in the office, the work of being a role model to your child's playmates, the work of being a patient spouse, the work of wonderful participation in God's creative hand.

This also means, of course, that we cannot be lost in our work to the detriment of the family. There are those who argue that "My prayer is my work" or "My worship is a job well done." No, no, no. We can be joyful at the opportunity to love Jesus in the little things done well and done with love, but we cannot believe that the little things can replace time with Jesus or time with our families.

There is a wonderful line in *Familiaris consortio*, also by Blessed John Paul II, which talks about the educative role of the parent. The pope teaches that no one, not one other person can ever fully replace the parent, and the parent can never fully delegate their role as a parent to another.[45] We are – no matter how poor a father or mother we might think we are – we are due to our children. They have a right to us. In our society, we easily forget the rights of children in this sphere. So to be just we must provide them with their due, their right to be with us and be loved by us. That too is part of the lesson of St. Joseph the Worker.

It is a great comfort to think that on particularly warm nights in Nazareth, as the cool wind began to ease onto their village, Jesus and St. Joseph went onto the roof of their home to escape the heat inside the house. St. Joseph, lying down, would have tucked his calloused hands underneath his head while the boy Jesus would lie next to him resting his own head on Joseph's arm.

Picture them both lying down to stare up at the sky and together silently wonder at the creation before them. At the end of a long day's labor, such repose would have been very refreshing for St. Joseph the Worker, especially as Mary's quiet song drifted up to them and filled their much needed night of rest with dreams of many more such evenings. No doubt the Father in Heaven looked fondly on the scene, in part because St. Joseph's faithful labor helped build the edifice of salvation. And no doubt that same Father looks kindly on the laborer today who sacrifices for his family and in doing so builds up the Kingdom of God.

St. Joseph the Worker, pray for us. Help us to understand the dignity of work and to learn how to better offer up our difficult work for the salvation of souls. Protect all families from undo harm, and teach us how to trust in the Providence of God through Christ our King.

Prayer

Dear Joseph, when we have a difficult day, frustrated with co-workers, clients, environment, career, wages pray that we can turn that frustration over to Jesus. Remind us that in doing the work well, despite the conditions, we might fulfill God's call for us. On our behalf, ask Jesus for the strength to stand up and speak out when there is real injustice.

Dear Joseph help us defend our co-worker who is treated as a mere thing. Help us speak up for the colleague who faces abuse and threats from his or her superior. Help us to lead with righteousness and follow with humility.

Help us give all our sufferings in labor over to Jesus, to Christ crucified. In those things that we cannot fix, help us to trust in him and offer up the situation. Pray that we might have the prudence to know when to speak and what to say. Help us to avoid bitterness and the anger that dehumanizes those around us. St. Joseph help us to entrust all things to God's Divine Providence just as you did so many times. Amen.

Compendium

220. *The sacrament of marriage takes up the human reality of conjugal love in all its implications* and "gives to Christian couples and parents a power and a commitment to live their vocation as lay

people and therefore to 'seek the kingdom of God by engaging in temporal affairs and by ordering them according to the plan of God'".[46] Intimately united to the Church by virtue of the sacrament that makes it a "domestic Church" or a "little Church", the Christian family is called therefore "to be a sign of unity for the world and in this way to exercise its prophetic role by bearing witness to the Kingdom and peace of Christ, towards which the whole world is journeying".[47]

266. *By his work and industriousness, man — who has a share in the divine art and wisdom — makes creation, the cosmos already ordered by the Father, more beautiful.*[48] *He summons the social and community energies that increase the common good,*[49] *above all to the benefit of those who are neediest.* Human work, directed to charity as its final goal, becomes an occasion for contemplation, it becomes devout prayer, vigilantly rising towards and in anxious hope of the day that will not end. "In this superior vision, work, a punishment and at the same time a reward of human activity, involves another relationship, the essentially religious one, which has been happily expressed in the Benedictine formula: ora et labora! The religious fact confers on human work an enlivening and redeeming spirituality. Such a connection between work and religion reflects the mysterious but real alliance, which intervenes between human action and the providential action of God".[50]

X

RUNNING LIKE ST. JOHN

It was Shaw who once said that "Youth is wasted on the young." The energy and drive of youth is not always properly matched with the single-mindedness or wisdom to know what is of value. That comes with maturity.

In the 1955 film "Rebel Without a Cause" we see youth in a comfortable, post-war America struggling to find a cause worthy of their youthful exuberance. In one scene, Jim, the new kid in town, and Buzz, the leader of the gang of local teenagers, discuss how a "chickie-run" works. They drive their stolen cars toward the precipice at high speed and then jump out. The first to ditch the car losses. It's a dangerous game between two rivals.

But Buzz tells Jim, "You know something? I like you." "Why do we do this?" Jim asks, not out of fear but out of genuine curiosity. With a kind of matter-of-factness that helps replace reason, Buzz answers "You've gotta do something. Don't you?" That line encapsulates the film. Without anything transcendent or vital in a world so comfortable, the young direct their energy to self-indulgence and mania.

But what if youth can be directed towards something truly grand? Insert the transcendent back into the lives of the young, and what becomes possible? Could they remind us of the purpose of life, the possibilities of hope and the idealism that perhaps we abandoned years ago? This is certainly part of the lesson of St. John.

In St. John the Beloved Disciple, the Evangelist whom we remember on December 27th, we see a young man who was single-minded and zealous like any young man. But his youthfulness was transformed by the transcendent. He too raced towards a precipice, but his cliff opened up to the all-encompassing love of God, a love that is never exhausted. His cliff was marked only by the limits of his heart.

St. John was driven by love, not by idleness. His love for Jesus was the example *par excellence* of the Christian attitude. He acted precisely in response to the urging of Christ's love. Almost nowhere else is the attitude of the true disciple better represented than by St. John himself in his own Gospel.

Easter Morning

Let us turn to the events of Easter morning, events which I have already touched upon earlier when reflecting on St. Mary Magdalene. There is much to learn from the beautiful detail with which John describes the events of that day. We read:

"So Peter and the other disciple [St. John] went out and came to the tomb. They both ran, but the other disciple ran faster than Peter and arrived at the tomb first; he bent down and saw the burial cloths there, but did not go in." (Jn 20:3-5)

What might St. John have been thinking as he ran? It is early in the day yet. Mary of Magdala had come to them in the locked room where they were hiding. Perhaps her showing up unannounced took them by surprise, but they were positively shocked when she said, "They have taken the Lord from the tomb, and we do not know where they put him."

St. John tells us that she had run to see them, so she was probably flustered, breathing heavily. Perhaps she was speaking in little bursts, words coming out in snatches as she tried to catch her breath at the same time. Maybe she had to repeat herself a few times before they understood what she had said. There was no discussion amongst the apostles about what should be done, about who should go or who should stay. Peter and John sprang up and ran.

St. Peter, who was not the agile lad that John was, still managed to muster a run. As he would have been a man past middle age, the running part suggests the urgency of the moment. John, however, is the younger man and is running faster, forgetting his older companion. The morning air may have still been crisp as St. John pushed himself to go faster and faster, the coolness of the air passing quickly across his flushed cheeks as he ran.

It may have been a lovely morning, dew clinging slightly to the olive trees' leaves and branches, but John is unaware of it for there is dread in his heart. *Where have they taken him?* He might be thinking. Mary of Magdala said "we," "we don't know." Did she check with some of the others in the community before she made it to the apostles? So no one knew what had happened? Where was he?

But maybe there is still hope in his heart. Perhaps the young John is running as hard as he is not because he is in dread fear that the Jews or Romans have stolen the body of the Master, his brother, his Lord but because there is hope that the Master is still alive. Perhaps, Jesus has performed another miracle, as he alluded he might. When one is as young as John, anything is possible.

At the same time, St. John was there three days before. Unlike the other Apostles, he witnessed the state of the body in all its horrifically contorted mess. He knew the suffering it underwent. He was there to comfort Mary, now his mother. He was responsible for her. He saw her quiet sorrow, quiet because every emotion had already been spent as they took Jesus down from the cross. Lord, what would he tell her now? Her son's body is now gone. They've taken that from her too.

Whatever the case, hopeful or in dread, John is driven on like a champion horse striving for the finish line. The goading is not in the switch of a rider, not in pain or fear of it but in the spurs of love. *I must see him. I must find him*, he says to himself. Anticipation fills the heart that powers John's legs, so he runs faster. That youthful exuberance, commitment and energy all find a place in John's heart as he strides forward seeking out the truth about Jesus.

Imagine the youthful John leaning forward as he ran, led not so much by his head but by his heart, chest thrust forward, legs struggling to stay underneath him so that he did not fall flat on his face. Perhaps he was not so much propelling himself but allowing himself to be drawn towards Jesus, surrendering to his youthful impulse to love whole-heartedly and with a purposeful singularity.

The Urgency of Christ's Love

We adore you, oh Christ, and we love you. Dear Jesus we do so love you. Give us the grace to pursue you as honestly, as heatedly, as passionately as St. John. We know that should we allow ourselves to love and be loved by you that the social Gospel of love for the poor can do nothing else but pour forth from our hearts. We know that by the urging of your love your Christian people will truly transform the world.

This attitude of running like St. John is the attitude for living the social doctrine. The social justice teaching of the Church sometimes leaves the Catholic cold with fear that they shall be asked to give up something perfectly good. *Why should we give it up?* We might think to ourselves. *There is nothing wrong in it.* So we play at token goods and make half-hearted starts towards serving others. Or perhaps we do serve the poor but relish in complaining about the pastor, the Church, the conservative fellow down the road or the liberal in the next pew.

But if we are running with the attitude of St. John, we are running for Christ. He will not allow us to do anything else but to give of ourselves in a spirit of love and for the sake of others. The passing beauty of the things of this world, the distractions of flickering blue lights on a screen, the fears, the pain, the mindless pastimes, the cruel words we enjoy uttering, they all pass away. When our eyes are focused on the road ahead that leads us to him, he will always point us towards service that fulfills us and makes us better despite the difficulty.

That service he chooses for us will differ for each soul. One Christian will be called to the mission field beyond. Another Christian will be called to the mission field within. Still another will be led to the quiet care for an aging parent, or to the sweet witness of nursing a newborn. These callings are disparate, but they must all be rooted in Christ, and they must be pursued with the urgency that St. John shows us.

We can discern our calling when we feel the urgency of his love in our hearts. If Christ is in the poor, the downtrodden, the alien, the weak, the sickly, the forgotten ones of our society, then the urgency will rise up and bid us to run. We need only to learn how to be sensitive to the impulse. This sensitivity comes in prayer. So action must first start in prayer, an attitude of prayer that keeps us open to Christ's promptings.

These promptings can happen at any time and in many forms, for Christ is in the grumpy co-worker, the prickly boss, the sad friend who flails about seeking love in every tryst. He is in the obnoxious teenager, in the overbearing mother-in-law and in the dodgy politician whom we feel forced to support. The urging of Christ's love can come at us during any moment of the day. To respond in love, with the yes that Our Lady used, is to participate in the social teaching.

But Christ is also in the immigrant seeking food for living and in the unborn, in the union worker and the entrepreneur who are both trying to earn for their family. He is in the death-row inmate and in the criminal who seeks to take from you what is rightfully yours. Knowing that he is there, in them, waiting for us, how can we turn our backs? Why wouldn't we want to give our all for Jesus' sake?

And we need not fear the road to which he calls us. Running like St. John is not to run with dread. Rather, run to the Christ who calls even now in this very moment. Trust that the Master is there, waiting for you in your neighbor, for unlike St. John in his Gospel, we know where Jesus is. We know the secret which was still just a hope in John's heart, opening ever so slowly. We know that Jesus is Lord, that he has won the fight, that we can be with him forever if only we keep our eyes on him and not distract ourselves with the trappings of this world.

Sometimes we are caught up trying to fix things ourselves. A socio-economic, political theology that tries to remake the meaning of the Christian project into a movement for social welfare has lost the point. The well-meaning humanitarian may be a stellar fellow, but such a fellow would not run to see Jesus. If he sought him out at all, he might only muster a slow-paced walk. The humanitarian who can do away with Christ and religion works too often out of anger and frustration and sometimes out of mere curiosity. Sometimes the humanitarian is motivated by love, but it is love for humanity and not exactly for human persons. It is love for the idea and not for the individuals. The urging of Christ's love helps us see the trees and the forest, humanity and the human.

Once we've found Jesus in the poor and our everyday neighbor what do we do? We can rant and rave about injustices. We can complain. But the saints do less ranting and more acting in love. Nowhere in St. John's Gospel do we have a single Apostle decrying the Roman occupancy. It was certainly an injustice, but Christ himself tells the Jews to give to Caesar what is Caesar's.

So, instead of the rant, we are called to press our head upon Christ's breast as John did and, with the confidence of his love, dare to carry that love forward to others. Everything in the Christian life is an exercise of accepting God's love for us, and he desires us all the more even now.

This centrality of Christ must always be remembered. Without it, everything else collapses, and the social teaching becomes stagnant atheist humanism. The urging of Christ's love is the answer, an urging that propels us to run like St. John.

At the Tomb

Once St. John arrived at the tomb he waited for Peter. He stood in wonderment, hopeful. The rock was pulled aside. The tomb was indeed empty. He peered inside, not daring to go in. He could see only the linens cast on the floor. How odd that the thieves would have left the linens. Could it be true? Had he risen as he said he might?

Running like St. John is an exercise in hope, in

the endless hope that, despite all our failings and limitations, a society of love is possible, that we are safe from any real harm, that we are held up by God's fatherly hand of love.

Once inside the tomb with St. Peter, John moved from hope to faith. He saw the truth. The linens were cast aside. The napkin placed upon the face of the dead Jesus was now neatly folded. This was no robbery. He is risen! The temple was destroyed and he rebuilt it. He is the Son of God. He is the long-awaited Messiah. It is all true after all, and now – well now John and Peter rushed out of the empty tomb, reported to Mary Magdalene what they saw, for she too followed behind St. John's running, and then they ran to tell the others.

Run to tell the truth of Jesus. Strive to share your faith in him. And run too to our Mother, Mary. The ache in John's heart about what to tell Mary about the body was now gone. He is risen! Mother Mary would see her boy again. So he ran back to the Apostles and to Mary.

Like the Christ child who no doubt ran to Mary whenever he fell, we too are encouraged to run to her with our bruises, our pains and sorrows, no matter how small. Like a good mother she wants to help us. She is patient like a mother is, willing to undo our little problems so that we can continue on and run like St. John. She will help direct us to love our brother and sister in the poor.

May we learn to turn to her more often.

St. John pray for us and long live Christ the King.

Prayer

Dearest John, intercede for us when we feel as though Jesus is distant from us. Remind us to turn to prayer. Lead us to the Scriptures which are the Word. Place us before the poor, the lost and forgotten so that we might serve them. Allow us to see Christ in our neighbor, our children and our spouse.

John, help us to remember that the Jesus who we seek is in those who need help. Remind us to direct our yearning for Jesus into a service for the poor. Help us to leave our fears and worries behind and to run to Jesus who is buried not in stone but in the hearts of the wounded persons in our community.

St. John help us to love Jesus more. Pray for us. Keep us close to Jesus just as you were at the Last Supper. Protect us from despair. Remind us to continue to run, always to run towards the Master. Amen.

Compendium

206. *Love presupposes and transcends justice*, which "must find its fulfillment in charity".[51] If justice is "in itself suitable for 'arbitration' between people concerning the reciprocal distribution of objective goods in an equitable manner, love and only love (including that kindly love that we call 'mercy') is capable of restoring man to himself".[52] *Human*

relationships cannot be governed solely by the measure of justice: "The experience of the past and of our own time demonstrates that justice alone is not enough, that it can even lead to the negation and destruction of itself...."[53] In fact, "in every sphere of interpersonal relationships justice must, so to speak, be 'corrected' to a considerable extent by that love which, as St. Paul proclaims, 'is patient and kind' or, in other words, possesses the characteristics of that merciful love which is so much of the essence of the Gospel and Christianity". [54]

207. *No legislation, no system of rules or negotiation will ever succeed in persuading men and peoples to live in unity, brotherhood and peace; no line of reasoning will ever be able to surpass the appeal of love.* Only love, in its quality as *"form of the virtues"*,[55] can animate and shape social interaction, moving it towards peace in the context of a world that is ever more complex....

XI

THE FAITH OF DOROTHY DAY

Servant of God Dorothy Day was a writer and social commentator who, in the early 1900's, leaned decidedly towards the socialist world-view. Drawn to the faith because – amongst other things – it was the faith of the poor and the working class in America, Day converted to Catholicism in 1927. She had been interested in it for many years, noting its teaching about the human person and the divine, but it was the birth of her daughter that proved the final impetus. In fact, she converted despite knowing it meant the end of her relationship with the man she loved, the father of her child.

In 1932, with an inner call to continue her work with the poor and working class but without knowing how to do it, Day met Peter Maurin, a Frenchman who had come to the U.S. through Canada and a man well versed in the social teaching of the Catholic Church. This teaching of the Church – sometimes called the social justice teaching – is a body of principles and doctrines taught by the Church since the beginning as a natural extension of the Gospel of Jesus Christ. It is a kind of moral theology directed at how we interact with our society as Christians.

In the nineteenth century, however, the Church began to articulate this extension of the Gospel more directly to modern understandings of labor and capital, citizenship and government, economics and workers' rights, ethics and the environment, family and poverty. Peter Maurin was an intelligent man who had read Pope Leo XIII's 1891 *Rerum novarum*, the document that started modern, Catholic social teaching. He was also aware of Pope Pius XI's 1931 *Quadragesimo anno* on the fortieth anniversary of *Rerum*. Thus it was that he would be a mentor for Dorothy Day.

The two of them, Day and Maurin, founded the Catholic Worker, a penny-a-piece periodical that defended the rights of workers and spoke of other injustices. They wrote in an unabashedly Catholic manner, rooted in the social teaching of the Church. The newspaper would grow into a movement with Catholic Worker Houses that took in the homeless. They were "houses of hospitality" that entrusted all things to the Providence of God. Dorothy Day, the convert and eventual third order Benedictine, would, through her example, end up teaching all Catholics how to live the faith in authentic love for the poor. Her example is significant enough that, recently, the U.S. Bishops agreed to advance her cause for beatification and canonization, with no one less than Cardinal Dolan being one of her staunchest advocates.

"Don't Call Me a Saint"

This is all rather ironic as Dorothy is famous for her line, "Don't call me a saint. I don't want to be dismissed so easily." It is a jarring statement. What could she possibly mean? Taken out of the context of the rest of Dorothy's life, it could mean that she did not care for the Church's understanding of sanctity.

It is not uncommon, then, for social justice advocates to ask "Why are we even talking about Dorothy Day as a saint. I mean, would she even ever have wanted that? Would it have mattered to her?" Without knowing the rest of Dorothy Day's life, it seems a reasonable question. But Day offers an insight into her understanding of sanctity that goes well beyond the trite phrase quoted above. Dorothy Day, who said "Don't call me a saint," also said:

> "We should look to St. Thérèse the Little Flower, to walk her little way, her way of love. We should look to St. Teresa of Ávila, who was not content to be like those people who proceeded with the pace of hens about God's business, but

like those people who on their own account were greatly daring in what they wished to do for God. It is we ourselves that we have to think about, no one else. That is the way the saints worked. They paid attention to what they were doing, and if others were attracted to them by their enterprise, why, well and good. But they looked to themselves first of all."[56]

Dorothy Day intimately understood the Church's meaning of sanctity. This is why she called us to look to the saints as models. What's more, she directs us to look at contemplatives.

St. Thérèse of Lisieux and St. Teresa of Ávila are not known for passionate speeches before throngs of laborers, or for organizing sit-ins and certainly not for overthrowing economic systems or undoing the political class. They were cloistered nuns. They rarely, if ever, left their convent or engaged in massive efforts to feed the poor. They lived supremely "impractical" lives of constant prayer. They really did "look to themselves first of all." They took the Gospel passage about the log in their own eye quite seriously. Their message to us, to all who want to work for social justice is, to reform yourself first. Others may follow and transform the world, but reform yourself first. These saints spent their time with eyes affixed on Christ Jesus and wrote to us about how to seek holiness. These, says Dorothy Day, are the people to whom we should turn at all times.

Where Social Justice Goes Wrong

This is an important lesson, because there has been a rather disturbing trend in some social justice circles. It starts by arguing that the Church has spent centuries canonizing men and women who are known for their quiet piety and interior grace but not recognizing the great heroes of social reform. The Church sees devotion to the next life as valuable for the spirit, but it does not also value the resolve for immediate political reform in favor of the poor. The Church chooses saints that serve the poor and engage in astounding charity but not persons who fundamentally reform the socio-economic machine that causes poverty. Therefore, so some argue, the Church needs to expand her sense of the holy. It needs to re-imagine what it means to be a saint.

These criticisms mean that sanctity has to be retooled so that belief in the divinity of Christ is optional and adherence to the teachings of the Church is a give-and-take proposition. The real measure of the holy, so some of these good people say, is concrete change in social structures. The goal is the undoing of systems. This, therefore, requires remaking the Church into an organ for political theology. Short of condemning entire governmental systems, charity, love, kindness and resolute care for the neighbor are just sentimental drivel. Social justice must mean socio-economic revolution.

Thus it is that these social justice advocates conclude with a pantheon of new saints, saints who are relevant to the struggle for liberation here, now, today. And so social justice programs exist today that eschew the traditional saints. Worse, social justice programs exist that openly deny the divinity of Christ Jesus. Jesus is portrayed solely as a liberator of an earthly oppression and nothing more. There is no salvation from personal sin. The only sin that matters is social sin, structural sin, the sins of industry and corrupt governments. Or personal sin is reduced to our cooperation with social sin. Jesus came to save the world from injustice. Your sins, says one popular social justice book, your sins are already forgiven you.[57]

Why do this? Why deny Jesus' divinity and do away with the question of sin? Some argue that talk about a divine Jesus or sin keeps us focused on heaven and distracts us from the poor here and now, as though there were ever any evidence that the deep yearning for life in Christ in heaven could distract us from loving our neighbor. Nevertheless, some all-too-easily do away with the divine Jesus. Jesus, as one theologian has put it, may have been God, but such an idea is not "useful" for the struggle for socio-economic justice in the real world today. Thus it is that some ignore the "Christ of faith" for a "Jesus of history," a political Jesus, a radical.

The measure of the Christian, in this new model, is the degree to which he or she models a political Jesus. The faith exists for social change here. A church that does not seek fundamental change to the social structures of society is no church at all, and the Christian who is not involved in the struggle fails their vocation.

As a result, the stories of those saints whose lives are stunning canvases upon which Christ's love is painted are considered cartoon characters meant for children not grown-up Catholics. Why bother with the story of St. Maria Goretti? How does her tale of woe and sacrifice help the poor today? St. Isidore may have been a bright fellow, but what does his life have to do with the contemporary needs of so many? St. Germaine's life may have been something of note in the old days, but why should her passivity towards an unjust society be a model for those who fight for justice? So St. Thomas More lost his head, why should that matter? It seems some who claim to love the poor don't see Dorothy Day's point at all.

What is Social Teaching?

The social teaching, she might have explained, is not a kind of mere social animism. It is not a Catholic version of well-meaning humanitarianism. It is much more than that, because it is an encounter of Christ with Christ. It is an opportunity for Christ to work in the world through us. And it is an opportunity for us to encounter Christ in the poor. This was the point of countless Catholic animators who worked with the poor like Dorothy Day but also her dear friend Catherine de Hueck Doherty.

Doherty was a champion for the poor and founder of the Madonna House Apostolate which serves the materially and spiritually poor. She too has a cause open for her canonization, and she agreed with Day that Christian social justice cannot be mere welfare. "Service without prayer," said Doherty at a Charismatic Renewal Conference in 1979, "is paternalism, social service work, something that the poor do not accept."[58]

Also, the social teaching of the Catholic Church is not a third way between the extremes of Capitalism and Communism. It is not a paradigm for deconstructing social structures. It is not a cudgel to be used to beat our wealthier neighbors over the head. It is not an excuse to ignore the spiritual needs of the poor. It is certainly not a trump card for the Democratic Party against the Republican. It is not about this or that system or political ideology. It is not about following a radical Jesus and his message of political upheaval. It is not even primarily about social transformation. Those who reduce it down to these things do the teaching and the Church which birthed it a disservice.

So what is the social teaching of the Catholic Church about? Dorothy Day understood, with the help of her friend Peter Maurin (for sanctity is seldom a private enterprise), that like the rest of the Church's teaching, the social teaching of the

Church is meant to get Catholics to heaven. The social teaching of the Church is an invitation to sanctity, to live lives just like those which I have included here in this book.

The social teaching of the Church is about Christ Jesus who did come to forgive sins. The social teaching is about all of Jesus, the human but most especially the divine. It is about our getting to know and love him so that, by growing in that love, we cannot help but to say yes to him when he calls. And the social teaching helps us understand that Jesus is always calling us to serve the poor, that he is always inviting us to love our neighbor and that the Church provides us with advice on how best to do that.

Once the social teaching is pitted in opposition against the rest of the Church's teaching, it ceases to be about and from Jesus and so ceases to help the poor. Furthermore, once the social teaching is pitted against this or that political party, or ideology or movement, once the social teaching ends up becoming about "winning" this battle or that fight, even in the name of helping the poor, it ceases to be about and from Jesus. Once the social teaching is about guilting people into action, berating faithful Catholics for "merely" praying, it ceases to be about and from Jesus.

"The Mass is the Work"

So what did Dorothy Day mean by telling us

not to call her a saint? I believe that Dorothy knew that some Catholics have the habit of looking at sanctity as a special calling not meant for the average person. Saints are dismissed out of hand by some as specially-gifted beings sent by God in order to remind us that he still exists. They get special graces not available to we-the-lowly. Sanctity is well and good for them but it is not for me. Day, I believe, was annoyed at the thought that someone would label her a saint and then forget her in that same instant as just one of those special people who has nothing to teach the average Joe.

The truth about Day was that she worked hard at her spiritual life. She insisted on daily Mass. Once, when a young man had joined the Catholic Worker Movement and had failed to attend Mass, Dorothy pointed out to him that he was hurting the work they were doing.[59] It must all be centered on Christ, after all. Day understood this clearly. She once told a group of prospective members of the movement that "The Mass is the Work."[60]

She attended Mass, she prayed the rosary daily, she prayed the Liturgy of the Hours, she went to Confession weekly, she steeped herself in the Church's liturgical life because she knew that this was the way to plug herself into the Mystical Body of Christ whom she was trying to serve. What better way to know your patient, the poor, than by becoming one with him through the Eucharist? How else to encounter Christ than by becoming intimately aware of his many disguises in the poor and in what appears to be bread and wine?

Dorothy Day is the great contemporary example of the Catholic who was unwilling to compromise on the teachings of the Church but who also insisted on that social justice work that gives some Catholics hives. She railed against any kind of violence. She fully supported unions and the rights of workers. She protested against nuclear arms. She did all of these things, but she also abhorred the welfare state. She criticized the New Deal. She was very comfortable with the idea of doing away with large, centralized governments, as humanity had lived without them for so long.

She was this seemingly contradictory person because she knew whom she served. She was no slave to a political party. She was not an ideologue. She was rather a subject of Christ. She served him and his Church. That's all she needed to know. She would be a great patron for our time since she would easily discomfit those too comfortable on the Left and those too comfortable on the Right.

We should follow her example since she never let herself be pulled in any direction by any party or president or ideology. We should look to our own prayer life and make sure that we have that in order before we seek to point out the splinter in the world's eye. We too should seek out the formation in the social teaching which she received from Peter Maurin and others. In short, we should pursue the sanctity that she did and which we find in the lives of those in this book. That is the surest way of achieve social justice and peace. We should pray to her and them all to help us follow Jesus with greater devotion and to be able to say long live Christ the King.

Prayer

Dear Dorothy, when we struggle with our prayer and with attention at Mass, help us to remember Christ Jesus who suffers on the cross and in the poor. When we receive Jesus at the altar rail, in the host, in the small sip of blood from the chalice, remind us of those who suffer from infirmity and loneliness.

When we are tempted to complain about the Church, or accuse her of failing to live up to our standards, remind us to reform our lives first. Pray that we learn not to seek to change the world so much as to change our own spirit. Draw us closer to the sacraments, as you were, so that we can better serve the Church, our families and the community.

Intercede on our behalf so that we might have the courage to seek Jesus in the poor, to serve not with an attitude of bitterness but with an attitude of joyful gratitude. Amen.

Compendium

32. *Meditating on the gratuitousness and superabundance of the Father's divine gift of the Son, which Jesus taught and bore witness to by giving his life for us, the Apostle John grasps its profound meaning and its most logical consequence.* "Beloved, if God so loves us, we also ought to love one another. No man has ever seen God; if we love one another,

God abides in us and his love is perfected in us" (1 Jn 4:11-12). The reciprocity of love is required by the commandment that Jesus describes as "new" and as "his": "that you love one another; even as I have loved you, that you also love one another" (Jn 13:34). The commandment of mutual love shows how to live in Christ the Trinitarian life within the Church, the Body of Christ, and how to transform history until it reaches its fulfillment in the heavenly Jerusalem.

490. *Peace is the goal of life in society, as is made extraordinarily clear in the messianic vision of peace: when all peoples will go up to the Lord's house, and he will teach them his ways and they will walk along the ways of peace* (cf. *Is* 2:2-5). ...It is then that peace will be lasting, because when the king rules according to God's justice, righteousness flourishes and peace abounds "till the moon be no more" (*Ps* 72:7). God longs to give peace to his people: "he will speak of peace to his people, to his saints, to those who turn to him in their hearts" (*Ps* 85:9). Listening to what God has to say to his people about peace, the Psalmist hears these words: "Steadfast love and faithfulness will meet; righteousness and peace will kiss" (*Ps* 85:11).

Endnotes

1 John Paul II, Encyclical Letter *Laborem Exercens*, 22: *AAS* 73 (1981), 634.

2 John Paul II, Encyclical Letter *Centesimus Annus*, 36: *AAS* 83 (1991), 839.

3 Gordan Zahn, *In Solitary Witness: The Life and Death of Franz Jägerstätter* (New York: Holt, Rinehart and Winston 1964) 33. It should be noted that Franz did monetarily care for the child until the mother married another man.

4 It is interesting to note here that Jägerstätter did not publicly berate the bishops for their support of the Nazis. He wrote that members of the Nazi Party should not be allowed to receive Holy Communion in Austria, just as they had been barred in Germany for a time. Still, he countered that we should not "cast stones at our bishops or priests. They, too, are men like us, made of flesh and blood, and can weaken.... One cannot easily visualize for himself, therefore, the serious decision forced upon our bishops and priests in March, 1938." Ibid., 214-215.

5 Ibid., 42.

6 Ibid., 233.

7 Ibid., 33.

8 Ibid., 66

9 Ibid., 243

10 Ibid.

11 John Paul II, Encyclical Letter *Centesimus Annus*, 48: *AAS* 83 (1991), 854.

[12] Second Vatican Ecumenical Council, Pastoral Constitution *Gaudium et Spes*, 79: *AAS* 58 (1966), 1103.

[13] Cf. *Catechism of the Catholic Church*, 1741.

[14] Cf. John Paul II, Encyclical Letter *Veritatis Splendor*, 87: *AAS* 85 (1993), 1202-1203.

[15] John Paul II; Encyclical Letter *Redemptoris Missio*, 11: *AAS* 83 (1991), 259.

[16] Herbert J. Thurston, S.J. (ed.) and Donald Attwater (ed), *Butler's Lives of the Saints: Volume III* (Allen, Texas: Christian Classics 1996) 50.

[17] James Monti, *The King's Good Servant but God's First: The Life and Writings of Saint Thomas More* (San Francisco: Ignatius 1997) 53-54.

[18] Thurston *Butler's Lives of the Saints: Volume III*, 54.

[19] Cf. John Paul II, Encyclical Letter *Evangelium Vitae*, 73: *AAS* 87 (1995), 486-487.

[20] Cf. Congregation for the Doctrine of the Faith, Instruction *Donum Vitae*, (22 February 1987): *AAS* 80 (1988), 70-102.

[21] John Paul II, Post-Synodal Apostolic Exhortation *Christifideles Laici*, 39: *AAS* 81 (1989), 466.

[22] Cf. John Paul II, Post-Synodal Apostolic Exhortation *Christifideles Laici*, 39: *AAS* 81 (1989), 466.

[23] Cf. John Paul II, Post-Synodal Apostolic Exhortation *Familiaris Consortio*, 42-48: *AAS*74 (1982), 134-140.

[24] Thurston *Butler's Lives of the Saints: Volume III*, 342.

[25] Ibid., 343.

[26] Ibid., 344.

[27] Cf. *Catechism of the Catholic Church*, 2187

[28] Thurston *Butler's Lives of the Saints: Volume III*, 29.

[29] Cf. John Paul II, Post-Synodal Exhortation, *Christifideles Laici*, 39: *AAS* 81 (1989), 466-468.

[30] Cf. John Paul II, Message for the 1996 World Day of Peace, 2-6: *AAS* 88 (1996), 104-107.

[31] Herbert J. Thurston, S.J. (ed.) and Donald Attwater (ed), *Butler's Lives of the Saints: Volume IV* (Allen, Texas: Christian Classics 1996) 630.

[32] Ibid., 633

[33] Ibid.

[34] Day *On Pilgrimage*, 18-19.

[35] John Paul II, Encyclical Letter *Centesimus Annus*, 36: *AAS* 83 (1991), 839.

[36] Ibid.

[37] Cf. John Paul II, Encyclical Letter *Centesimus Annus*, 37: *AAS* 83 (1991), 840.

[38] Herbert J. Thurston, S.J. (ed.) and Donald Attwater (ed), *Butler's Lives of the Saints: Volume II* (Allen, Texas: Christian Classics 1996) 27.

[39] Quoted in Henri De Lubac, S.J., *Catholicism: Christ and the Common Destiny of Man* (San Francisco: Ignatius Press 1988) 55.

[40] Second Vatican Ecumenical Council, Declaration *Gravissimum Educationis*, 1: *AAS* 58 (1966), 729.

[41] Cf. John Paul II, Apostolic Exhortation *Familiaris Consortio*, 43: *AAS* 74 (1982), 134-135.

[42] Cf. Second Vatican Ecumenical Council, Pastoral Constitution *Gaudium et Spes*, 52: *AAS* 58 (1966), 1073-1074.

[43] Second Vatican Ecumenical Council, Pastoral Constitution *Gaudium et Spes*, 61: *AAS* 58 (1966), 1082.

[44] Brian Kolodiejchuk, M.C. (ed.), *Mother Teresa, Where There Is Love, There Is God* (New York: Image 2010) 45.

[45] Pope John Paul II, *Familiaris consortio* para. #36

[46] John Paul II, Apostolic Exhortation *Familiaris Consortio*, 47: *AAS* 74 (1982), 139; the quotation in the text is taken from Second Vatican Ecumenical Council, Dogmatic Constitution*Lumen Gentium*, 31: *AAS* 57 (1965), 37.

[47] John Paul II, Apostolic Exhortation *Familiaris Consortio*, 48: *AAS* 74 (1982), 140; cf.*Catechism of the Catholic Church*, 1656-1657, 2204.

[48] Cf. Saint Irenaeus, *Adversus Haereses*, 5, 32, 2: PL 7, 1210-1211.

[49] Cf. Theodoret of Cyr, *On Providence*, *Orationes* 5-7: PG 83, 625-686.

[50] John Paul II, Address during his Pastoral Visit to Pomezia, Italy (14 September 1979), 3:*L'Osservatore Romano*, English edition, 1 October 1979, p. 4.

[51] John Paul II, Message for the 2004 World Day of Peace, 10: *AAS* 96 (2004), 120.]

[52] John Paul II, Encyclical Letter *Dives in Misericordia*, 14: *AAS* 72 (1980), 1223.

[53] John Paul II, Encyclical Letter *Dives in Misericordia*, 12: *AAS* 72 (1980), 1216.

[54] John Paul II, Encyclical Letter *Dives in Misericordia*, 14: *AAS* 72 (1980), 1224; cf.*Catechism of the Catholic Church*, 2212.

[55] Saint Thomas Aquinas, *Summa Theologiae*, II-II, q. 23, a. 8: Ed. Leon. 8, 72; cf.*Catechism of the Catholic Church*, 1827.

[56] Quoted in *On Pilgrimage*. Dorothy Day, *On Pilgrimage* (Grand Rapids, Michigan: Eerdmans 1999) 20.

[57] Albert Nolan, *Jesus Today: A Spirituality of Radical Freedom* (New York: Orbis Books 2006) 83-84. Fr. Nolan goes on to assure us that God's relationship to the world is like that of our souls to our bodies and that the Earth itself is alive. Nevertheless, his book was used by a prominent social justice program as *the* example of a spirituality for social justice.

[58] From an address to the Eastern Catholic Charismatic Renewal Conference in Atlantic City, NJ 1979. Audio accessed at http://www.discerninghearts.com/?s=Catherine+Doherty on March 29, 2013.

[59] Quoted in *On Pilgrimage*,17.

[60] Ibid., 37.

Made in the USA
Columbia, SC
08 January 2024

30081145R00114